ULTIMATE HAPPINESS MASTERY

In 5 Simple Steps

Discover Happiness Enemies, the Truth behind Lies, and Learn How to Live a Happy Life at Home and Workplace with Time-Tested Skills and Secrets of Mindful-Meditation, Positive Emotions, Flow, Responsibility-Accounting and Resiliency in All Situations and Circumstances.

AJAY PRABHU

<u>A beautiful **GIFT** to my readers</u>

<u>*Claim your FREE eBook:*</u>

HAPPINESS for all age groups by Ajay Prabhu

(Don't miss this FREE eBook)

<u>*Send your contact details on:*</u>

https://forms.gle/Hc2mcAPeiUC MqTNt8

<u>I will send you</u> my FREE eBook to your email.

Copyright Page

Ultimate Happiness Mastery in 5 simple steps book is copyright protected and is only for personal use. You cannot reproduce or duplicate, store in a retrieval system the content of this book, cannot transmit through a form of a book, digital form including application or pdf, amended, distributed, sold, resold, used, quoted, or paraphrased without the direct written permission and consent of the author or publisher.

Efforts are put to ensure the reliability and accuracy of the information in this book. The reader is responsible for all liability and negligence or otherwise due to any use, misuse, or abuse of any information, methods, steps, ideas, strategies, tactics, etc., contained in this book.

Under no circumstances the author or the publisher will be holding any blame or legal responsibility either directly or indirectly, personal or otherwise.

Disclaimer Notice

Please note the information contained within this book is meant for making an attempt to solve happiness problems.

The reader agrees to make his own decisions and consult a licensed professional if need be.

The reader agrees that the author would not be responsible under any circumstances for any consequences after reading and applying the skills, techniques, methods, etc., or any knowledge provided in this book.

The reader agrees that the book is aimed at providing education and entertainment and not for rendering any consulting services or professional advice.

All the information is presented "as is" without warranty or guaranty of any kind.

Acknowledgments

I thank all those who gave me knowledge and experience during my interactions with them in my ups and downs in life.

I want to thank my parents, elders, peers, younger ones, spiritual teachers, scriptures, family members, and friends with deep gratitude for building a solid foundation for my happiness journey.

My special thanks to my teachers and coaches for teaching me and helping me to bring out the author hidden inside me in the form of this book.

I wish to give full credit to my students and clients for working and cooperating with me to apply inputs for success and happiness.

Last but not the least, a huge thanks to Amazon for making my dream of becoming a self-published author come true in a very systematic and professional way.

Dedication

I dedicate this book to the Higher Self, who helped me to control my monkey mind and earn me the title of HAPPINESS CONQUEROR.

I also dedicate this book to my readers who have taken a bold step to initiate their first step towards living a happier life by transforming themselves.

Table of Contents

Chapter 5: Simple lies about Happiness

Chapter 6: Simple truths about Happiness

Chapter 8: Happiness Gems of All Chapters 205

Chapter 1: Introduction

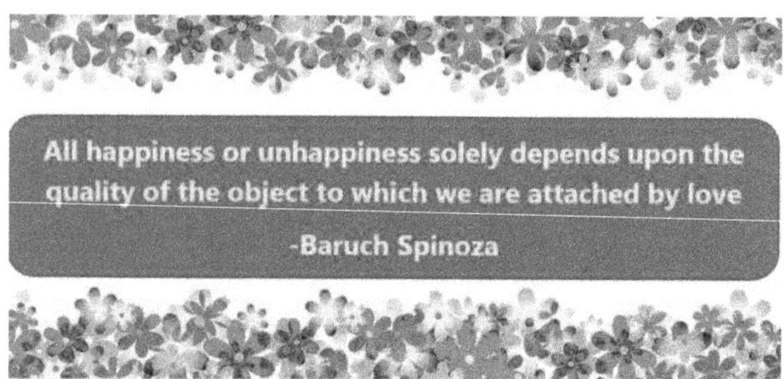

Ultimate Happiness Mastery in 5 simple steps is my first book in the Let's Enjoy Happiness series.

Congratulations on taking action towards your first step of happiness.

Welcome to the quest of seeking long-lasting happiness wisdom, entirely relevant in today's times.

The sand beneath our feet slips after the ocean's rising waves strike us and return to the ocean. Similarly, have you noticed that the strong waves of ups and downs in life make you feel sometimes happy and sometimes sad?

Many of you may complain that there are only a few occasions to smile. The chaos & sorrows in both the inner and outer world inundate us.

We waste precious time facing personal struggles; one knows nothing about where, when, and how to find happiness.

Did you ever find the need to pay attention to this vital aspect of life and attempt to learn how to find happiness in all walks of life?

Do you have a desire to discover a new vantage point in happiness and experience bliss in life?

Happiness is one of the largest searched words by over 7 billion people of the world right from when they were born until they exited this world.

Yet, very few people will come up to the fore and confidently say that they are completely happy.

I always wanted to understand the true meaning of happiness and find a way to become happy in any circumstance and situation.

Like many people, I tried to search for happiness by reading various books, taking guidance from national and international happiness experts, and all other possible methods.

With immense efforts and perseverance, the long-lasting happiness idea sparked my mind, and suddenly, life started appearing more meaningful.

I understood the essence of happiness and meaningfully reflected, churned, ingrained, and molded happiness into my lifestyle.

The application of all this learning in my real life while dealing with thousands of people throughout my life helped me design my happiness formula. It also helped me to discover a brand-new perspective of life.

It motivated me to share this secret formula with all of you to find the real meaning of happiness and to enjoy happiness in every moment.

I have provided you with curated, and distilled knowledge and wisdom gathered from many years so that you don't get lost in the bulky pages.

I will focus on the essential points of happiness that will help you understand and implement them better.

My readers of this book will be able to relate to their enemies of happiness and master the art of winning the war against enemies of happiness.

I am sure that this book will be useful for people of all ages to find the real meaning of happiness and live a happy life with intentional and permanent happiness.

Your journey to a happy life can begin in just one step i.e. Read this book.

Start your happiness journey by reading this book and learn to be always happy.

I intend to bring many more flavors of happiness in my next books in the Let's Enjoy Happiness series.

Please look out for it to continue your Happiness journey and experience longer and longer-lasting happiness.

All the Best!

Ajay Prabhu

Your Happiness Coach & Evangelist

✓ Start your journey of happiness by reading this book and learn to be always happy.

Chapter 2: Why should we discover and conquer the enemies of Happiness?

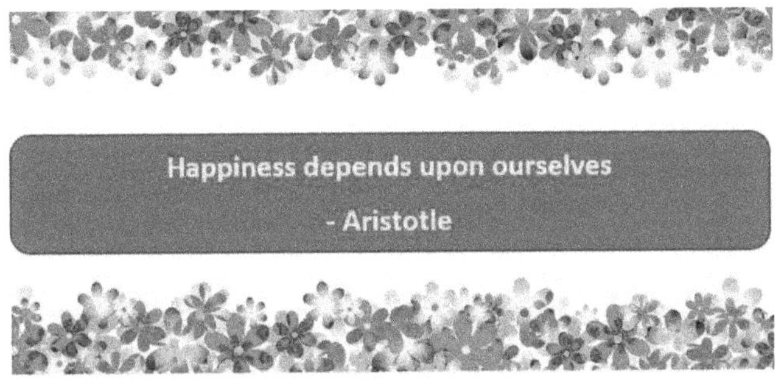

Are you happy all the time?

Can you remain happy in all situations and circumstances?

Do you know the enemies of happiness? Do you know how to conquer the enemies of happiness?

Well, If the answer to all the questions as mentioned above is "No," then this is a must-read chapter before we dive deeper into understanding every minute detail about happiness and the time-tested steps to remain happy every moment of our life.

I am sure you want to enjoy long-lasting happiness in every aspect of your life. I, too, strongly believe that the very purpose of life is to seek happiness. Every person born on this earth wants to be happy and aims to derive pleasure and joy from most of his/her activities.

I keep on traveling to different places. I like to be with nature and soak myself into it. These solitude moments help me find answers to special questions of my life.

How I was questioned on Happiness?

One day, I was sitting over the shining golden sands on a Goa beach. My eyes were trying to penetrate the ocean, and my ears were quietly listening to the relaxing sound made by the ocean waves. My inner mind was savouring the happy moments I had in my life.

Suddenly, my mind asked me a very simple yet thought-provoking question "Are you happy"?

I wanted to give an immediate answer" Of course, Yes."

But my inner mind again poked a new question "What about the moments in which you are unhappy."

I thought for a while and was convinced to believe that I was not happy all the time.

The honest answer to the question of my inner mind was a "Yes" as well as "No."

I was a bit confused and wondered about the reasons behind the two different answers. I did not expect the answer to such a simple question could be in" Yes" as well as "No."

Now it was my turn to ask a question to my inner mind.

I asked my inner mind, "What could be the reasons for the unhappy moments in life?"

My inner mind quickly replied, "Entertainment of the enemies of happiness rather than destroying of the enemies of happiness."

The reason behind the mass unhappiness is people are not aware of the enemies of happiness.

I was astonished to know this surprising truth of happiness from none other than but from my inner mind.

I started feeling nervous and wanted to do something to conquer the enemies of happiness. I got some relief in the following quote:

"Pay attention to your enemies, for they are the first to discover your mistakes."

- Antisthenes

I was happy to note that the enemies of happiness need not be searched outside the mind but within the mind.

The best part of this search is the mind itself helps you by becoming your friend rather than your enemy.

Did you also feel the same?

Are you also able to relate to my unique experience on the biggest questions on happiness?

Does your inner mind also give the same answers? What do you say? Do you want to say a big yes, then after reading this book, you will be able to train your inner mind to remain happy all the time and answer your happiness questions in Yes and Yes always.

Every person born on this earth can be happy every moment of their life and enjoy all the precious gifts provided by God.

We all come into this world suddenly from the womb of our mother and grow further with the inputs provided to us, care taken for us, and experiences gained by us.

Despite all knowledge, skills, and abilities imbided by us, there is no guarantee that it will help us to unravel the secrets to live a happy life every moment of life, irrespective of our age, situations, and circumstances in life.

Our mother gives birth to us, and she pushes us out of her womb against our wishes. We try to find reasons for all those things that do not happen the way we want from our birth.

We immediately lodge our protest to our mother, with a big cry. The love showered by our mother gives us both comfort and relief.

A small incident that made me realise the natural state of happiness.

Recently, I met a six-month-old baby, whom I was supposed to meet after his birth six months before. Due to the Corona pandemic, I had to postpone my happiness meeting with him.

As soon as the baby saw me, the baby first responded with a confused look, with wide-open eyes, asking itself who this guy was?

"He is neither my father nor my mother."

"He is also not my grandfather nor my grandmother."

"Why is he trying to cajole and talk sweetly to me?"

In turn, I was eagerly waiting for a big smile on his face, but I had to wait till the happiness hormones were generated with my tons of positive emotions showered upon him.

And finally, the baby flashed a big smile, and it went ahead to the extent of communicating with me in his language of aha's and ahu's.

I felt so happy! I can't describe this happiness in words.

I was also a baby once upon a time and was surely happy in my natural state of mind. So is every human being as everyone has to pass through the childhood stage.

In spite of being happy and knowing the art of being happy from such a tender age, why most of us have forgotten this art and science of happiness?

As we grow older, we struggle to hold on to this blissful state.

The enemies of happiness start attacking us, and we begin the most extensive search of our life: to identify the worst enemies of our happiness.

We begin to ask our parents, teachers, friends, trees, toys, dogs, cats, and all those entities; we come across one fundamental question: Who is stealing and destroying my happiness?

Since we cannot get a clear answer from anyone, we have to find the answers to our happiness questions by ourselves.

Research says that at least 8 out of 10 people are unhappy, and 3 out of 10 people can enter the stage of depression.

"How to become happy" is one of largely searched question on google.

Based on our research, we do succeed in getting some good answers to this big question of our life.

However, we cannot afford to do a full-time Ph.D. on happiness. Our intense and hectic schedule forces us to get back to work until the same or new enemy of happiness once again strikes us and makes us unhappy.

You might have lost your job!

Your business might have slowed down and smashed heavy losses!

You might have broken relationships!

The Covid pandemic might have put a big lock on business plans!

Your boss may have more demands due to working from home!

You might be struggling to get promotions!

Your girlfriend/ boyfriend might have ditched you!

Your kids may not be listening to you, or your children may not produce the results you want!

You might have been struck with grief by losing your near and dear one and not sure how to continue your life journey!

You might want the world to listen to you and give you everything you desire.

How to get everything to become happy?

If one could have a magic wand to get everything, one can never be unhappy.

Your problem is getting worse day after day, and you don't know how to get everything you want and become happy in life.

The pursuit of happiness becomes more complex with more achievement – be it wealth, status, promotion, success, comforts, luxuries, etc.

I will help you in your pursuit of happiness.

No need to worry now. No waiting time now.

You don't have to get worried if things are not going your way.

I will teach you how to be happy, in spite of not having everything you desire.

I will make you realize the power of satisfaction and contentment to stay happy for a longer period.

I have minutely observed the vicious cycle of happiness to unhappiness for infinite times since my childhood.

I, too, have also experienced the frustration of not finding the keys to happiness.

Like everyone wants to be happy, I also want to be Happy.

But the ups and downs in life, sudden setbacks during happy moments of life were acting as stoppers to my otherwise successful life and were always baffling my mind.

I was always having a feeling of why some bad things happen after good things.

I intensely wanted to know how to overcome the attacks of enemies of happiness.

I was not sure whom I should ask and when will this unhappiness end.

I tried reading books, consulted experts, and had to spend lots of time, money, and energy to get a perfect fit for my problems and a magic stick to keep me happy.

I decided to do a serious study on happiness and found out the root causes of unhappiness.

How did I conquer the enemies of happiness?

With a focused approach and mindful thinking, I have succeeded in conquering the enemies of happiness.

In this happiness journey, I have discovered specific tools, techniques, strategies, and tactics to defeat the enemies of happiness.

Why am I sharing my secret tools, techniques, strategies and tactics to defeat the enemies of happiness?

Looking at my Happiness, many people around me became eager to know the secrets of Happiness.

I shared all my secrets of Happiness with them. The results were fabulous, and I was told the tools, techniques, strategies, and tactics are very powerful and could solve problems of different types of people.

People who used my tools, techniques, strategies, and tactics to defeat the enemies of Happiness could learn to become happy at home as well as workplace. Their mind was filled with peace, and they could also spread Happiness with people around them.

Now I want to reveal all these tools, techniques, strategies, and tactics to you all to win this ultimate war of our life.

Your search for long-lasting Happiness is now over, as I am going to manifest a simple and easy step-by-step approach to become happy and stay happy for as long as you want.

I will teach you everything about Happiness, including the what, why, how, where, when, who and which of Happiness essential for earning the precious designation of a happiness conqueror.

I will reveal to you the astonishing secrets, techniques, tools, strategies, and tactics to become happy every moment, irrespective of, in what situation, circumstances you are in, and **WITHOUT spending a bomb on costly consultations and programs**.

I will reveal everything; I have gathered in over 30 years to master the Art of Happiness.

I will teach you where to find Happiness and keep it with you for a longer time.

In your pursuit of Happiness, my treasure of Happiness will work as a lighthouse to spread bright enlightenment in every aspect of your life.

You will also learn to make this world a better place to live in and accomplish success in every endeavour.

You will master your happy life and live the life you want.

- ✓ The enemies of happiness start attacking us, and we begin the most extensive search of our life: to identify the worst enemies of our happiness.
- ✓ Since we cannot get a clear answer from anyone, we have to find the answers to our happiness questions by ourselves.
- ✓ We do succeed in getting some good answers to this big question of our life.
- ✓ Our intense and hectic schedule forces us to get back to work until the same or new enemy of happiness once again strikes us and makes us unhappy.
- ✓ The pursuit of happiness becomes more complex with more achievement – be it wealth, status, promotion, success, comforts, luxuries etc.
- ✓ With a focused approach and a mindful thinking, I have succeeded in conquering the enemies of happiness.

- ✓ You should have no worries now about the enemies of happiness, as I am going to share my secrets, techniques, tools, strategies and tactics to become happy every moment, irrespective of, in what situation, circumstances you are in and WITHOUT spending a bomb on costly consultations and programs.
- ✓ Your search for long lasting happiness is now over, as I am going to manifest a simple and easy step-by-step approach to become happy and stay happy for as long as you want.
- ✓ I will teach you everything about happiness, including the what, why, how, where, when, who and which of happiness essential for earning the precious designation of a happiness conqueror.

Chapter 3: What is Happiness?

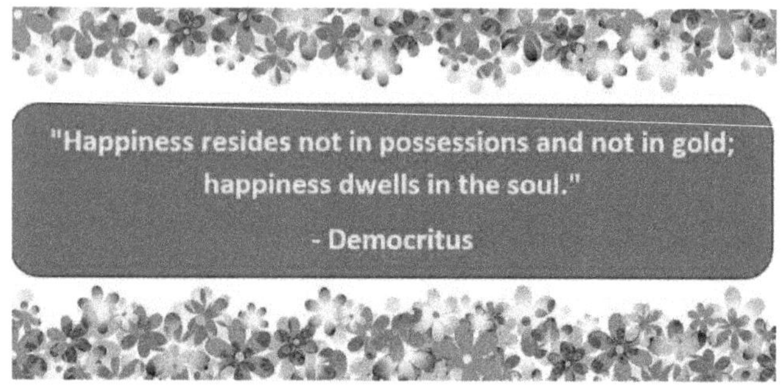

Have you heard about the story of a fisherman and a business tycoon?

The story goes as follows:

Once upon a time, a business tycoon visited his ancestral home near a beach to enjoy his vacations.

He went to the beach early morning at 6 am and saw a fisherman busy gathering his catch for the day.

The fisherman was very happy as he had trapped a big shark fish in his net and was trying to separate it from other small fish.

The business tycoon was amazed to see the happy fisherman enjoying his big success for that day.

He wanted to increase the happiness of the fisherman and asked the fisherman if he could give him the advice to increase his happiness.

The fisherman was surprised at the question of the business tycoon and replied, "What advice do you want to give me to increase happiness."

The business tycoon gave a big smile and further asked the fisherman, "What is his cost-benefit analysis for his fishing business? i.e., how much effort is required by him for making a small profit for his livelihood."

The fisherman replied, "Sir, I spend about 2-3 early morning hours and could gather a catch that can help him create a livelihood for a couple of days."

The business tycoon carefully listened to the fisherman's answer and, after introducing himself, expressed his desire to suggest to become a business tycoon like him by expanding his fishing business.

The fisherman was surprised and curious to know about the suggestion offered by the business tycoon.

However, his mind alerted him and convinced him that he was happy with his daily activities and did not wish to do anything more.

Since the fisherman did not want to kill the business tycoon's helping gesture, he allowed the business tycoon to let him know the suggestion.

The business tycoon was very happy to note the fisherman's response and requested him to narrate all the activities done by the fisherman, right from waking up in the morning to going to bed in the night.

The fisherman then tells all his activities, right from waking up in the morning to the early morning fishing activity. He further explains selling fish, buying vegetables, and other essentials for the family. He finds time to play with his kids and takes a small nap in the afternoon. He goes for a walk in nature with his wife in the evening, doing anything he likes like singing, dancing, painting, and finally retiring his day after dinner with a good sleep at night.

The business tycoon immediately jumps into a happy gesture and says, "Here you are."

"I can certainly help you to expand your business and become happier."

"The only thing you have to do is to follow my advice sincerely."

The business tycoon is convinced about his expansion cum happiness plan for the fisherman. He suggests he buy a bigger fish catching boat to go into deeper oceans to gather a more significant catch for earning more and improving his lifestyle.

After listening to the business tycoon, the fisherman is puzzled. He inquisitively asks the business tycoon about the need to get himself so busy, stress complete, and anxious by doing all suggested by the business tycoon.

The fisherman confidently replies, "When I am already happy with what I am doing and am thoroughly enjoying my life, why should I do something different and face the risk of stress, anxiety, destroying my family life and free time?"

The fisherman further states that he had already done that before but found himself chasing happiness not enjoyable in the present times. Since he wanted to be happy now and remain satisfied in the future, too, he has trained his mind to enjoy happiness in the present.

The moral of this story, happiness is a choice for every human being.

Every human being can enjoy his natural state of happiness until he does something silly that makes him unhappy.

Happiness is a state of mind wherein a person experiences a feeling of joy, contentment, satisfaction, pleasure, etc., and finds meaning in every activity in the process of living a life.

They understand the meaning of happiness provided to us by Mahatma Gandhi.

"Happiness is when what you think, what you say, and what you do are in harmony"

- Mahatma Gandhi

Happiness does not mean a life without problems, stress, and anxiety. Everyone has to face problems, stress, and anxiety in particular life situations and circumstances. A happier person knows the art of remaining joyful despite the difficulties, stress, and anxiety.

What is happiness?

Happiness is a feeling which is experienced within and determined by one's state of mind.

Internal as well as external events can impact the state of mind.

Success in gaining some material things may result in a temporary feeling of pleasure, e.g., buying a new car.

Failure to lose some worldly stuff may result in a fleeting sense of sadness, e.g., not getting a hike in salary.

However, in between the times when there is no success or failure, our mind adapts itself to a neutral level of happiness.

So, happiness has two extremes in ecstasy on one end and frustration on the other end.

In the neutral state, we are neither pleased nor frustrated and still claim to be happy.

This neutral state may vary from person to person, based on genetics, perceptions, satisfaction or contentment levels, moment-to-moment responses to the events unfolding in life, and circumstances and situations of life.

Even then, as Mahatma Gandhi has said, a happy person creates happiness when what he thinks, what he says, and what he does are in harmony.

A happy person is no exception. He, too, has to face problems in life, become stressed, and feel anxiety due to challenging situations and circumstances.

Every human being goes through the ups and down roller coaster at his home or workplace.

However, a happier person knows the right way to dilute the impact of negative emotions and challenges and succeeds in every situation and circumstance to enjoy happiness every moment.

Who wants to become happy?

I have a strong feeling that every living, as well as a non-living entity on our planet Earth, wants to be happy.

Every entity has its own way of perceiving happiness and enjoying happiness.

We have heard incidents about a child inside the womb of the mother expressing happiness, a new born child demonstrates his happiness on birth, children have their own way of enjoying happiness, teens have refined methods of enjoying happiness, the married, retired, and super elderly persons too have defined patterns of happiness.

An unborn child enjoys a cozy environment in the womb of his/her mother. As soon as he/she comes into this world, he/she cries to announce his arrival. He/she has to adjust himself or herself to the new atmosphere outside the womb of the mother.

Ask a small child, "What will make him/her happy."

He/she will immediately shoot a quick answer, "Lots of toys and play time."

Ask a teenager, "What will make him/her happy."

He/she will immediately shoot a quick answer, "Pleasure and joy in good relationships and social connections."

Ask a married person, "What will make him/her happy."

He/she will immediately shoot a quick answer," Each other's love and focus on each other's strength."

Ask an unmarried person / single person, "What will make him/her happy."

He/she will immediately shoot a quick answer, "Self-love and enjoying life on their terms."

Ask a retired person, "What will make him/her happy."

He/she will immediately shoot a quick answer, "Accept life as it is with limited resources but plenty of wisdom."

Ask an elderly person in their super 80's and beyond, "What will make him/her happy."

He/she will immediately shoot a quick answer "There is nothing more to achieve except union with God and savouring every joyful moment created with his/her near and dear ones."

No one is wrong. Each one has their way of expressing happiness, and that's all okay!

Every person has a right to enjoy happiness the way they want. However, if they follow the social norms, they can also make society equally happier.

The moment-to-moment responses will differ with the unique and contemporary experiences gathered by the infant, and so will be their satisfaction and contentment levels.

The feelings of satisfaction and contentment may change with different circumstances and situations.

But the fact of the matter is comparisons fail, as every moment creates a new event and situation.

New situations and circumstances will produce a unique feeling of satisfaction and contentment for every moment.

We cannot be happy by living in comparison, but by living in the present moment and enjoying the present moment.

One can easily win a battle over comparisons by feeling grateful for all the things we have and comparing ourselves with those who do not have what we have.

This change in perspective can quickly increase our satisfaction and contentment levels.

Happiness is our birth right as we are all born happy. Don't you see a small child always smiling? However, the magnitude of our happiness decreases with the inputs we receive as we grow.

Our parents, teachers, friends, and guides try to develop a growth mindset within us.

We start believing that happiness depends on material gains. When these beliefs get hardened into attitude, we unconsciously fall into the trap of enemies of happiness such as desires, fear, anger, greed, lust, etc.

Ultimately, we forget our real blissful nature and begin a new search in pursuit of happiness.

Our search begins with buying and reading various books on happiness, taking guidance from happiness coaches, and spending a bomb transforming ourselves from an unhappy person to a happy person.

Very few people succeed in finding the right course at the right time. Others continue their pursuit of happiness.

Traditional European societies often linked Happiness with morality and have inherited happiness principles from the Greeks and Christianity.

Protestantism and Capitalism later redefined Happiness in lesser terms of social life and more in individual psychology.

Utilitarian's comprising the western ethics side preferred ethical behaviour for becoming happy.

Eudaimonia: Aristotle popularised the concept of Eudaimonia, which means doing all the good things for living a happy life. Western cultures prefer individual Happiness.

Plato had stated that people who have morals could live happy life.

Democritus emphasized cheerfulness for living a happy life.

Hedonism: Hedonism claims Happiness in maximizing pleasures and minimizing pains. Democritus popularised the concept of Hedonism. The true hedonist would aim at living a meaningful life. It may also involve self-control for reducing the pains, which may limit the pleasures.

Authentic Happiness is a fusion of Hedonic (feel-good pursuit of pleasure) and Eudemonic (a deeper kind of contentment coming from a sense of meaning, personal growth, and self-actualization) to experience the natural flow of life.

The Nordic countries such as Finland, Norway, and Demark are ranked in the top happiest country in the world by the United Nations World Happiness Report. They have high-quality free healthcare and education. They devote time to family, provide generous maternity and paternity leave, monthly child allowance until a specific age, productive efforts at the workplace, better environment for citizens and outdoor setting in the lap of nature, etc. to live a better life.

World Happiness Report 2021

Subjective well-being relies on three leading indicators: life evaluations, positive emotions, and negative emotions.

Gallup World Poll is the principal source of data to evaluate subjective well-being.

Ranking of happiness (average life evaluations) based on the 2020 surveys

(Top 10 countries)

Country name	Score,2020	Rank by 2020 score
Finland	7889	1
Iceland	7575	2
Denmark	7515	3

Switzerland	7508	4
Netherlands	7504	5
Sweden	7314	6
Germany	7312	7
Norway	7290	8
New Zealand	7257	9
Austria	7213	10
India	4225	92

Happiness concept of Eastern countries:

The **Advaitian's** from the Indian subcontinent believe that the ultimate goal of life is Happiness. The Vedanta school of Hindu philosophy states that Ananda (Happiness) is the top state of unification of an individual with God after becoming free from all desires, physical and mental ordinary pleasures, sins, and sufferings.

The **Dvaita Vedantians** (based on a reading of the Bhagavad Gita) believes that Ananda as Happiness is experienced by good thoughts and good deeds with sound mind control. One can reach the state of supreme Bliss in all walks of life with evenness of temper and mind.

The **Vishishtadvaita Vedantians** believe that real happiness can be achieved through divine grace after the surrender of one's ego to the Divine.

Ramana Maharshi's teachings say that Happiness is within and can be known only through discovering one's true self.

Swami Vivekananda has an important take on Happiness: Both Happiness and misery dilute the existence of our true blissful nature, i.e., Higher Self – the atman.

With the existence of our blissful soul, we don't have to get anything as we have everything. Freedom from desires can make a person live a life with enduring Happiness.

The **Buddhist** teachings say that Happiness can be achieved with the noble eightfold path (right view, right resolve, right speech, right conduct, right livelihood, right effort, right mindfulness, and right samadhi) for ultimate freedom from suffering.

Self-observance, self-restraint, kindness and compassion, and reducing cravings of all forms can lead a human being to ultimate Happiness.

The Chinese Confucian thinker **Mencius** believed that giving priority to a moral self and great virtues than physiological or lower self will help to lead a happy life.

The **Judaists** believe that Happiness lies in the service of God. Their spiritual text links Happiness and joy in the context of the service of God.

Taoists believe that Happiness is based on following nature rules and living a healthy and contented life and not on the luxuries or power of worldly life.

In **Stoicism**, human beings can be happy by manifesting virtues and accepting what they have, and making the best use of it by living in the present.

Self-control and fortitude can be used to destroy negative emotions without getting impacted by the desire for pleasure and fear of pain.

A human being should understand their role given by nature and work together by treating them in a fair and just manner.

Sonja Lyubomirsky, distinguished American professor of psychology and famous author of the bestseller "The How of Happiness: A Scientific Approach to Getting the Life You Want," states that Happiness is the experience of joy, contentment, or positive well-being, combined with a sense that one's life is good, meaningful, and worthwhile.

Sonja Lyubomirsky has also provided a 50-10-40% formula for determining Happiness.

The 50-10-40% formula devised by Sonja Lyubomirsky, a well-known researcher in Happiness, explains why some people are happy while others are not happy. According to her 50-10-40% formula, our Happiness is determined by Setpoints (50%), Circumstances (10%), and Intentional activities (40%)

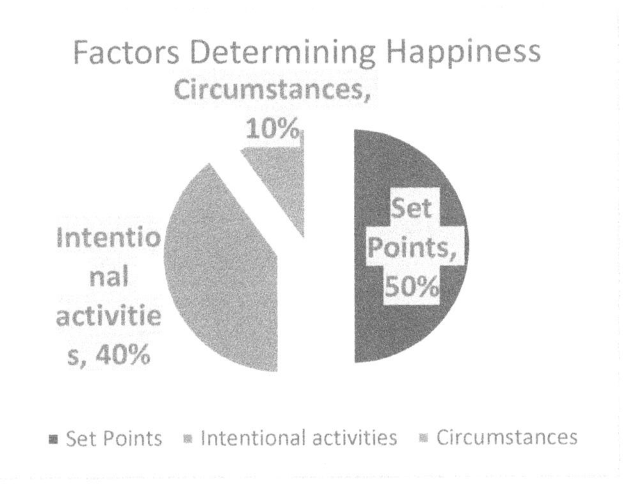

 A human being can control some of these factors that affect happiness while others cannot be controlled for e.g.

Set points =Genes = 50% = (cannot be controlled)

Circumstances such as income, marriage, looks, etc. = 10 % (can be controlled)

Intentional activities and influence = 40% (can be controlled)

Dr. Martin Seligman (considered as the father of positive psychology) and his team studied positive emotions and their impact on Happiness on human beings.

Seligman introduced the Authentic Happiness theory in 2002 and found that Happiness depended on three distinct dimensions of human life, i.e., positive emotion, engagement, and meaning.

Each of the dimensions is measured in terms of life satisfaction through a subjective report.

According to Dr. Seligman, Happiness has three dimensions: the pleasant life, good life, and meaningful life.

Pleasant life can be realized by enjoying basic pleasures of life such as needs of human beings, the natural environment, etc.

I liked the Dr. Seligman approach as it hits the root of unhappiness, i.e., negative emotions. Negative emotions such as fear, anger, hatred, etc., are dangerous as they create a win-lose game. Positive emotions can help us to create a win-win game.

Human beings can have thoughts that will have a positive impression about the Past, Present, and Future.

Positive emotions of the Past

- ✓ Satisfaction
- ✓ Contentment
- ✓ Fulfilment
- ✓ Pride
- ✓ Serenity

Dr. Seligman suggests using the time-tested weapons of forgiveness and gratitude to combat negative emotions and unhappiness.

Positive emotions of the Present

- ✓ Joy
- ✓ Ecstasy
- ✓ Calm
- ✓ Zest
- ✓ Flow

Dr. Seligman suggests using the time-tested weapon of mindfulness to increase Happiness in the Present by being in the flow.

Positive emotions of the Future

- ✓ Awe
- ✓ Hope
- ✓ Optimism
- ✓ Faith
- ✓ Trust

Dr. Seligman suggests using the time-tested weapon of hope and optimism to resist depression and perform better in challenging circumstances.

Here, I would like you to make a specific note about the super attributes of the Higher Self. The Higher Self is all powerful and succeeds in all situations with positive emotions.

The moment negative emotions creep in, we need to identify ourselves with the Higher Self. Automatically the positive traits and emotions of the Higher Self will be imbibed in us, and we can create a win-win game as positive emotions are frequently paired with happy situations.

Dr. Seligman and Dr. Christopher Peterson have established the linkage of good character with lasting Happiness.

The good life can be experienced by discovering our unique strengths and virtues and using them creatively to enhance our life experiences.

Dr. Seligman extols the functions of strengths and virtues against unhappiness and its supplementary use to build resilience. He has very beautifully stated the ubiquity of six virtues in his book: Authentic Happiness.

In a cross-cultural study with his team, and after examining and researching various religious and philosophical texts from all over the world, Dr.Seligman and the team have identified six virtues that were valued in almost every culture.

The six attainable virtues are:

1) Wisdom & knowledge
2) Courage
3) Love & humanity
4) Justice
5) Temperance
6) Spirituality & transcendence

Dr. Seligman makes a very important revelation of the role of strengths to achieve the virtues in our life. He strongly asserts that the strengths of the character are the route to achieving the virtues in our life.

The twenty-four signature strengths identified by Dr.Seligman in his book: Authentic Happiness are as follows:

Wisdom and Knowledge

1. Curiosity

2. Love of learning

3. Judgement

4. Ingenuity

5. Social intelligence

6. Perspective

Courage

7. Valor

8. Perseverance

9. Integrity

Humanity and Love

10. Kindness

11. Loving

Justice

12. Citizenship

13. Fairness

14. Leadership

Temperance

15. Self-control

16. Prudence

17. Humility

Transcendence

18. Appreciation of beauty

19. Gratitude

20. Hope

21. Spirituality

22. Forgiveness

23. Humor

24. Zest

Dr. Seligman strongly recommends the development of signature strengths for achieving virtues in our lives and leading a good and happy life.

Happiness is derived from different sources as every human being is different. Hence, we need to develop different attributes of Happiness available from different sources of Happiness that can make a person happy.

For e.g., someone may find Happiness in buying a luxury car, while others may derive Happiness from a world tour.

Human beings cannot always remain happy from external sources of Happiness. A wild chase for deriving Happiness from external sources makes him a rat in a rat race of Happiness.

The total Happiness can be derived from within when the mind turns inward. Once a person is able to control his mind, body, and intellect, he/she can easily experience long-lasting inner bliss. The control on the mind can be achieved by peeling off the layers of ignorance.

Since Happiness is a subjective experience, it is also referred to as subjective-well-being

A Meaningful life can be experienced with a deep sense of fulfillment with the help of signature strengths and virtues for a purpose greater than ourselves.

For living a meaningful life, Dr. Seligman takes the idea of flow conceptualized by his contemporary and colleague Mihaly Csikszentmihalyi. He advocates using the concept of flow to get engaged in acts of altruism and of kindness to experience greater levels of Happiness.

Abraham Maslow had described the well-being concept with the characteristics of a self-actualized person.

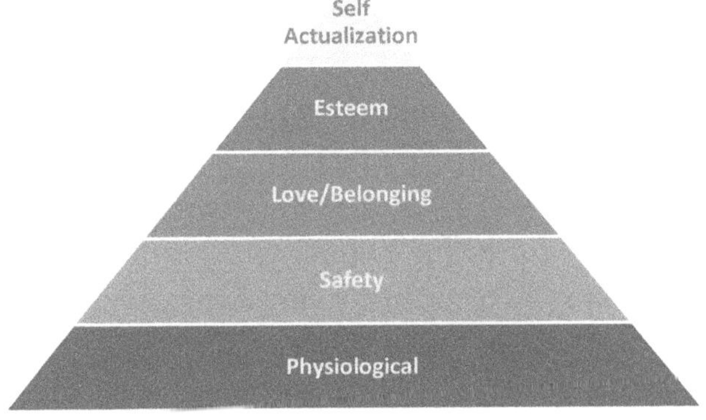

As per Maslow's theory, an individual will first like to fulfill lower-level needs starting from Physiological and move upwards towards Safety, Love, Esteem, and finally Self Actualization.

The basic needs include food, water, air, sleep, etc., come at the bottom of the pyramid as physiological needs.

After fulfilling the physiological needs, most people prefer safety and security to have greater control over life. It can include physical security, emotional security, financial security, etc.

The need for love and belonging encourages a human being to network for enhancing social relationships.

After establishing social relationships, a human being desires to have respect from others which can enhance his self-worth and status in society.

Finally, in the self-actualization state, human being desires to attain full utilization of their talent, capability, and potential.

However, Dr. Martin Seligman went one step further to explain the characteristics of a flourishing and thriving individual with his PERMA model.

Dr. Seligman's PERMA model has five elements that can help people to work towards a life of fulfillment, happiness, and meaning.

The five elements of Dr. Seligman's PERMA Model on Happiness are as follows:

P – Positive Emotion: Positive emotions about the past, present, and future can create a good feeling to help people enjoy the daily tasks in their lives, inspire people to be creative at work, and persevere with challenges by remaining optimistic about the outcome

E – Engagement: Absorbing oneself in the current moment by fully deploying their skills, strengths, and attention helps oneself to find calm, focus, and joy. It also floods the body with positive neurotransmitters and hormones that create a blissful immersion into the activity called "Flow." Acts of altruism and kindness motivate the signature strengths to be in others' service by losing self-consciousness.

Mihaly Csikszentmihalyi, the co-founder of positive psychology, introduced the concept of "flow" to enhance happiness levels. He states that flow is created by voluntarily stretching a person's body or mind to a limit to achieve a challenging but worthwhile task. The flow enhances the happiness levels of people doing such difficult tasks.

R – Relationships: Maintaining good relationships with near and dear ones, friends, and coworkers at the office can amplify love, intimacy, and a strong emotional and physical connection. Acts of kindness directed towards others are central to adaptation and help an individual to give purpose and meaning to life. It also increases well-being as well.

M – Meaning: Finding meaning in actions to serve someone bigger than the self keeps people engaged in enriching others' lives; for e.g., parents find meaning in improving the lives of their children. Happy people find meaning at the home, office as well as in social relations.

A – Accomplishments: Goal setting aligned with the Vision and Mission of life helps us to check results and provide a sense of accomplishment. Accomplishments offer satisfaction for the efforts put in to get the desired results. Such visible achievements not only ensure fulfillment in life but also encourage others to thrive and flourish.

Happiness Formula

Dr. Martin Seligman also gets the credit for providing the happiness formula.

Dr. Seligman's happiness formula is:

H = S + C + V

Where;

H = Enduring level of happiness

S = Set range

C = Circumstances in our life, and

V = Factors under our voluntary control

H = Enduring happiness level: Momentary levels of happiness can be increased by instant gratifications such as sweets, flowers, toys, etc. However, the real challenge is to increase the endurance level of happiness. Happiness due to instant gratifications tends to decrease with an increasing number of pleasures. As soon as the strength of the gratification evaporates, the happiness levels also diminish. One can measure the momentary level of happiness with the Fordyce Scale and Sonja Lyubomirsky's General Happiness Scale.

S = Set range: We have seen from Sonja Lyubomirsky's determination of happiness formula that we can control about 50% of our happiness as the remaining 50% depends on our genes. Hence our happiness gravitates in the set range.

C = Circumstances in our life: One can change his/her adverse circumstances or purchase luxurious comforts to increase happiness. It may cost him dearly, but it will be purely an individual's choice

V = Factors under our voluntary control: One can change the enduring levels of happiness by injecting positive emotions in the past, present, and future.

Happiness Ratio by Dr. Barbara Frederickson

Dr. Barbara L. Fredrickson, a well-known Professor of Psychology, has done detailed research on positive emotions, which significantly impacts the science of happiness. Positive emotions like love, gratitude, joy, etc., play an essential role in personal well-being. Negative emotions lead to fear, anger, frustration, etc. Her research on positive emotions states that a positivity ratio of 3:1 is ideal for personal well-being.

Where do we find happiness?
We don't have to dig huge mountains nor engage ourselves in any adventurous activities to seek happiness.

Even though the external factors can provide us pleasure and generate the happiness hormones within ourselves, we can generate the happiness hormones without the external materials.

Happiness is a positive emotion created within ourselves by our self. Long-lasting happiness can be experienced with the help of specific positive emotions such as satisfaction and contentment.

The best part of satisfaction and contentment is it makes our happiness independent of material pleasures. It trains our minds to remain happy under all situations and circumstances and eliminates the possibility of mental disturbances.

In the present context, especially in the 21st century, happiness should be a careful blend of eudemonic wellbeing with a full, meaningful purpose in life and hedonic wellbeing with the right balance between pleasures and living a good life of virtues without any overdoing.

When do we find happiness?
We don't have to look for a special time or occasion to be happy.

Happiness is the ultimate goal of our life, and hence we should learn to be happy every moment.

Since we have to face life as it comes, we need to be mindful while doing our activities. If we put our best efforts into not worrying about the regrets of the past and the anxiety of the future, we will learn to live in the present moment and enjoy Happiness, irrespective of the results or complications in life.

Best focused efforts will always produce excellent results. Happiness goal continues to be our main goal in life as Happiness is enjoyed in the journey of life rather than achieving small milestones in life.

What are the benefits of happiness?

Aristotle, the famous Greek philosopher, has wonderfully defined the unique benefit of Happiness.

According to Aristotle, Happiness is the meaning and purpose of life, which means our ultimate goal in life is to be happy. But the point is what benefits we will get by becoming happy.

The first important benefit of Happiness is it helps us to enjoy a healthy life with a strong immune system, a lesser risk of damage, and the misfunctioning of body organs such as the heart, kidney, lungs, etc., due to stress and anxiety.

The second important benefit of Happiness is the creation of positive emotions, which helps us to become more productive at home as well as the workplace, builds long-lasting relationships, inculcates good habits of eating, exercising, timely and adequate sleep, relaxing and enjoying recreations, etc.

The third important benefit of Happiness is developing self-control and self-awareness, which enables every happy human being to make the best use of their potential without blaming and criticizing others for failures. In fact, a happy person masters the art of resiliency and can bounce back from any setback in life.

Happy people become more successful in life and are able to accomplish all life goals.

The fourth important benefit of Happiness is the utilization of gratitude and forgiveness attitude for thanking and appreciating all the good things given by God and forgiving all those who have intentionally or unintentionally caused harm to any person.

The art of gratitude helps the person to remain contented on what one has, and at the same time focus on the present to make the best use of the available opportunity.

Forgiveness and letting go help the person to stay away from the negative energy of regret, criticism, jealousy, and comparison in order to preserve 100% positive energy on the activity on hand.

The fifth and the most important benefit of Happiness is maintaining a peaceful mind in all situations and circumstances and living a simple life filled with virtues for being useful to others.

Happiness promotes wellbeing and fulfilment of life goals. Happy people have increased life longevity and reduced pains while dealing with failures and setbacks in life.

Happy people are problem-solvers and better decision-makers and hence are trusted and liked by all.

Since they win over people on all fronts, they not only acquire leadership roles but are also able to generate adequate wealth for themselves as well as for their near and dear ones. Happy people remain prosperous in life.

Happy people love to be in touch with nature and persistently feel they are a part of nature.

This feeling inspires them to perform every transaction of their life with the power of the Higher self rather than a lower self.

Since they always work with true intention and compassion, they always remain favourites of the universe, which in turn creates luck and miracles for the happier persons.

"Happiness is not something ready-made. It comes from your own actions." – Dalai Lama

With this chapter, we can conclude that happiness is a feeling which depends on internal and external factors.

The external factors may not provide the same intensity of happiness over time and may force the happiness seeker to look at some other object to provide happiness.

However, if one remains contended with what one possesses and focuses his energy on fulfilling his meaningful goals, he/she would not be dependent on external factors. Instead, one can easily create happiness within and make others happy also. Hence happiness is an inside-outside approach.

An individual who wants to be happy has to depend on external factors for survival.

The essential needs have to be satisfied up to a certain extent. Happy individuals should learn to maintain a balance between Hedonic and Eudaimonia approaches to happiness.

The clarity in happiness has improved with research over time. Dr. Martin Seligman's PERMA Model on Happiness is useful for individuals and institutions.

One can also understand the factors determining happiness with the 50-10-40 formula provided by Sonja Lyubomirsky and take proper actions to improve his/her strengths and virtues, which can create more positive emotions and more prolonged lasting happiness.

We can certainly focus on 50% of the factors under control and enjoy the setpoint's bonus to enhance our happiness. Life is never constant and indeed filled with ups and downs. An ideal positivity ratio of 3:1 helps us to train our minds that even though there may be some negativity we may face due to circumstances and factors beyond our control, we can remain happy.

- ✓ Happiness is a choice for every human being.
- ✓ Every human being can enjoy his natural state of happiness, until he does something silly that makes him unhappy.
- ✓ Happiness is a feeling which is experienced within, and determined by one's state of mind.
- ✓ Happiness has two extremes in ecstasy on one end and frustration on the other end.
- ✓ In the neutral state, we are neither pleased nor frustrated and still claim to be happy.
- ✓ A happier person knows the right way to dilute the impact of negative emotions and challenges and succeeds in every situation and circumstances to enjoy happiness every moment.
- ✓ Every entity has its own way to perceive happiness and enjoy happiness.

- ✓ We cannot be happy by living in comparisons, but by living in the present moment and enjoying the present moment.
- ✓ Happiness is our birth-right as we are all born happy.
- ✓ Happiness is expressed in different ways by different schools of thought.
- ✓ Even though the external factors can provide us pleasure and generate the happiness hormones within ourselves, we can generate the happiness hormones without the external materials.
- ✓ Long lasting happiness can be experienced with the help of specific positive emotions such as satisfaction and contentment.
- ✓ Happiness is the ultimate goal of our life and hence we should learn to be happy every moment.

Chapter 4: Who are the Enemies of Happiness?

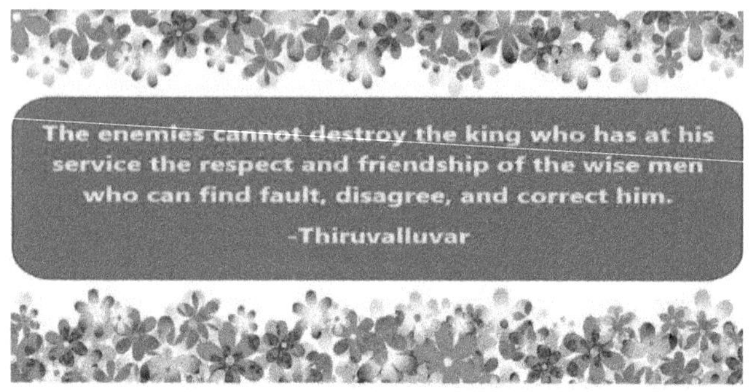

Story on enemies of happiness

Let me introduce you to a King, and his delighted Kingdom. The King retired due to a severe injury in a war, and his only son, who was 18 years old, was made the King.

The prince had to step into the shoes of his successful father immediately, but he was not prepared to take up sudden responsibility.

Other kings desired to capture this prosperous Kingdom but could not do so because of the stronghold of the erstwhile king.

The prince had a wise minister who gave timely advice to the King. Looking at the immaturity of the prince, he guided the prince to identify his enemies and prepare himself and his army to have proper controls on them.

Even though the prince was immature and inexperienced, he had firm faith in his ministry and had an open mind to understand whether the suggestion given by the minister was good for him and his Kingdom.

Based on the suggestion, the prince planned strategies to have a good relationship with the nearby friendly kings and took all possible steps to get rid of the enemy kings.

As the Prince grew older, he could develop more strategic techniques and methods to improve his relationships with the nearby friendly kings and took all possible steps to eliminate the enemy kings.

The prince soon became the strongest King of that region, and all the nearby Kings started respecting him and took shelter from him. Due to the tremendous success of the prince turned to King, his entire Kingdom was happy and remained prosperous for a longer time.

Friends, this story depicts the Kingdom we have created with our body organs. Some of these body organs are visible to us, while others are invisible. Each part of our body is responsible for creating happiness and sustaining happiness for us.

We come into this world suddenly on our birth and try to cope with the situations and circumstances thrown at us during our life journey.

Some of us get proper guidance and training to deal with the ups and downs in life, while most of us are on our own to identify the enemies of happiness and then devise tools, techniques, strategies, and tactics for conquering the enemies of happiness.

Like the Prince, we need to trust someone and take guidance to win this biggest war of life. We may have to bring expertise from many tutors and coaches, yet we cannot win all the battles of life. I have minutely observed the granular details of the vicious cycle of happiness responsible for converting our happy life into unhappy life for infinite times since my childhood.

We should prioritize listing all these causes of disturbance of peace and happiness and call them enemies of joy. Once we make a list of happiness enemies, we should attack them one at a time so that our focus becomes very strong against these enemies. Since we attack them one at a time, each enemy becomes the No. 1 enemy for that moment of attack.

Your worry about identifying the enemies of happiness is over now. I have listed out all the enemies of happiness in this chapter and will explain how to overcome the five worst enemies of happiness.

 So let us understand these enemies of happiness in this chapter before we embark on our journey of finding a way to be happy every moment.

Who are the enemies of happiness?

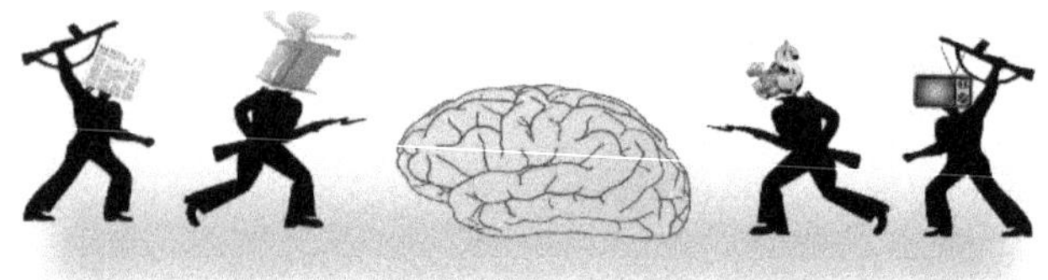

25 enemies of happiness

The main enemies of happiness are as follows:

1. Mind

2. Ego & foolish identification with body

3. Ignorance & incorrect beliefs

4. Bad choices & Values

5. Wrong Desires

6. Wrong Virtues (Unacceptable behavior showing poor and not high moral standards.)

7. Bad thoughts not aligning with higher self

8. Negative emotions & feelings

9. Attitude of blaming and criticizing others

10. Non-Optimistic and gloomy feeling

11. Lack of Mindfulness

12. Laziness and procrastination

13. Unclear vision and goals

14 Wrong Habits

15. Ingratitude

16. Fear

17. Anger

18. Anxiety

19. Getting broke easily without Resilience

20. Hurt and Pain

21. Lack of humor and fun in life

22. Greed

23. Jealousy & comparisons

24. Gossip

25. Not letting go and not forgiving

Now let us analyze the 5 worst enemies of happiness.

1. Jumping Mind

Our mind can become our great friend in times of need and our enemy when we need it the most.

Just like the King, the mind has to serve us rather than control us.

If we have to control our mind we have to act like a King and manifest the attributes and qualities of the King.

I know it is not easy, but every person has to make a beginning to learn new things to either dilute or eliminate the weakness.

Lord Sri Krishna has beautifully described the importance of controlling the mind for mastering life in chapter 6 of the holly Bhagavad Gita. He insists to have control of mind for attaining peace and happiness in life.

John Milton, a distinguished English poet has rightly said that the mind can make a heaven of hell or a hell of heaven.

How can our jumping mind become our enemy?

The mind jumps from one thought to another without any reasoning and logic and does not let us distinguish between a good deed and a bad deed.

It confuses us and forces us to make a wrong decision.

The mind on its own is bound to jump from one thought to another, but we are responsible for giving birth to a jumping mind.

The enemy mind enjoys the freedom given to it and makes us run after unending desires. We are forced to run a race that does not have a finishing line.

When we drive on a highway that has no destination, we are bound to run out of fuel and break down after some time. Instead of choosing our right path and the destination, our jumping mind takes us for a wrong mis-adventurous drive, whose ultimate destination is the destruction of peace and happiness.

We need to train our minds by constantly letting them know the goal and the purpose of our life. Once the mind is clear with our goals and purpose in life, it is bound to generate thoughts that are aligned to our goals and purpose in life.

We can easily train our minds with mindful meditations and periodic positive affirmations.

As soon as we feel the slipping of the mind from the focused thoughts to the non-focused thoughts, we have to awaken our higher self and remind the mind of useless thoughts.

Once we do this, the lower self will find an exit from our mind, and the jumping mind can be transformed into an obedient mind for generating the right thoughts for the right feelings, actions, and results.

Mindful meditation will first bring our disturbed and confused mind to a neutral and peaceful level.

The mindfulness aspect will fix the mind on our pre-decided vision and goal and focus our thoughts on the right actions.

The affirmations will constantly remind the mind about our vision and goals and will put it on alert as soon as any non-focused thought tries to enter our minds.

<u>**Weapon to destroy the Jumping Mind**</u>: Transform your Jumping Mind to Mindful Mind.

2. Ego

Dissolve your ego before it dissolves yourself.

- Maxime Lagace

The ego is invisible and is believed to be the shadow of the self. The ego develops with age and experience. Egocentric people develop an attitude of superiority over others.

The ego has the capability to act as an invisible enemy of our happy life. The ego entertains desires aimed at enjoying material pleasures and openly demonstrates anger, stress, anxiety, loneliness, non-co-operation - when things don't happen the way they want.

Ego can blur our self-image and shut the doors of positive emotions such as love, kindness, friendship, compassion, mindfulness to our mind. Egoistic persons can even go to the extent of harming others if their demands are not fulfilled. Ego can make a person stubborn and spoil healthy relationships.

An inflated ego can stop improvements in successful people and may stunt their career growth.

Researchers say that ego identifies itself with our lower self and takes credit for every little thing that happens in our life.

It distorts our higher self by making us forget that we are just a small participle in this huge creation created by the creator.

It generates ridiculous expectations and makes us hungry for validation from external entities. Egoistic people blame others for their setbacks and failures and find faults in others to make them feel superior.

By pampering the ego, a happy person can ruin and destroy his/her peace of mind and happiness.

A person who wants to get rid of ego should learn to check the signs of ego before the ego becomes uncontrollable.

A controlled ego can shower various benefits on the happy person, such as it will encourage the person to listen to others advice, build confidence rather than overconfidence, not to fall prey to the praise of others, embrace humility rather than pride, learn the art of celebrating success without comparing the results with others, and in case of low feeling get inspired to face any type of challenges head-on.

Since ego develops over time and age, it needs to be destroyed tactfully. An antidote to ego is self-awareness.

Self-Awareness means identification with the real Higher Infinite Self and not the limited lower self.

Self-Awareness exhibits completeness and stops one from running after short-term gratifications.

An egoistic person can be trained to remain contented and competent with ego-less action.

The only way to destroy the ego is by shifting from a doer-ship attitude to a do for the God attitude.

The absence of pride calms the mind and keeps away all the agitations that emerge from the doer ship attitude.

We then become the instruments in the hands of God and remain happy every moment in whatever we do.

Six sure-fire steps to reduce or drop the ego

I have identified six steps to reduce or drop the ego.

Step 1: Forgive others and let go of the hurt caused to you intentionally or unintentionally.

Forgiveness and a letting go attitude shall keep you happy and cheerful by eliminating negative energy.

Step 2: Be generous in helping others after fulfilling your basic needs with simple living. Focus on life goals. The art of unconditionally loving others will help you to play your role provided by the creator by taking instructions from the Higher Self rather than a pampered ego.

Step 3: Practice Meditation to keep yourself grounded in the Higher Self and stay away from mental disturbances. Meditation will prepare you for the next step i.e. Mindfulness.

Step 4: Be Mindful while performing your daily activities and contribute 100% effort towards the activity based on your vision and goal. Mindfulness will increase your productivity and transform you into a helpful team player.

Step 5: Pay Gratitude by thanking God for all your achievements and good things in life. When you send positive vibrations to the Universe, you will get back more good things that are stored for you by the Universe.

Step 6: Replace Pride with Humility. Never take credit for the good things that have happened to you. Instead, offer the credit to God and thank the Universe for giving you an opportunity to perform an act efficiently.

Weapon to destroy the Self-centred Ego: Transform the Self-centred Ego to Self-less Ego

3. Fear

What is Fear?

Fear is a natural emotion that alerts us from danger.

Fear can be an important aspect of our life.

Because of fear, we learn to prevent ourselves from harm. For e.g., when we started to drink hot milk from a cup on our own, initially we burnt our lips.

Later we mastered the art of drinking warm milk by allowing it to lower the temperature. Just because of the fear of burning our lips, we did not stop drinking the milk.

Some people just don't do anything because of different types of fear, such as fear of failure, fear of making wrong decision, fear of imperfection, etc.

I would like to quote a famous quote by the Tibetan Spiritual Leader Dalai Lama, which states that **"Happiness is not something readymade. It comes from your own actions."**

The main point in this quote is we have to perform our actions without fearing the outcomes. Without actions, Happiness cannot happen.

Right from our childhood, we have been taught to develop a protective, fearful mind.

If we are not supposed to do anything, then we are reminded about the adverse consequence that will happen.

Instead of taking the right message from this alertness signal, many people have made this a part of every activity.

In spite of there being no immediate danger, people presume something untoward is happening in their minds and fail to do their activity on hand. Instead of enjoying the fruits of action, they lose all their energy with the negative thoughts of fear.

Yes, your mind will try to tell you about the danger in every activity, but we as masters of the mind should train it to keep away the unwanted taught of fear in every activity.

How can fear be an enemy of Happiness?
Fear can become an enemy of Happiness if we misuse the emotion of fear. Instead of utilizing the emotion of fear as a danger signal to remain alert and to perform our planned activity, if we postpone or don't do the activity on hand, we suffer anxiety and failure. Because of anxiety and failure, we become unhappy.

Fear stops us from responding when there is no danger at all.

Have you heard about the fear of failure? It is also sometimes called atychiphobia. The fear of failure can come when we are responding to a situation or circumstance. One big reason for fear is due to desire to become a perfectionist.

We don't complete an activity on hand till the outcome happens as per our desire. We don't let the activity happen because of the harm in the future due to some lacuna in our work.

Fear of failure destroys our Happiness by making our mind anxious, generates a feeling of helplessness, and drives us to avoid any activity on hand.

Even though you have the essential knowledge, skills, and ability, the fear of failure makes you believe that you don't have it or have inadequate knowledge, skills, and ability.

Fear of failure convinces you that you cannot achieve your goal to become productive and happy.

The worst part of the fear of failure is it eats away the most precious time due to procrastination.

When the fear of failure gets hardened into your mindset, you automatically have low expectations from yourself, and your team may not like you due to poor inefficiency and effectiveness.

Fear of failure shatters your confidence and fills worries in your mind about disappointing others due to your failure.

Fear of failure is responsible for lower self-esteem, poor self-motivation, disturbed mind with minimal concentration, feeling of guilt, and shame for not meeting your goals and performing the role assigned to you.

How can you overcome fear?

Reframe the fearful thoughts

The first step to overcoming fear is to reframe your thoughts. Tell your mind that nothing harmful is going to happen, just like a mother tells her growing child to keep the child away from the thought of fear.

Do a small meditation by focusing your mind on your Higher Self and breath steadily with a positive affirmation "I am the master of my mind. My mind listens to me and understands there is no harm in this action. My mind has come to a neutral state. Now I can do my activity on hand peacefully, without worrying about any harm or danger."

This step has helped me a lot to face fear head-on.

Focus on your goal

Once the disturbed mind and confused mind are transformed into a peaceful mind, focus on your activity which you can perform with your knowledge, skills, and abilities.

Be prepared for anything happening due to your mistake. Be prepared for the outcomes as they can always be improved. Don't let negative emotions enter your mind by thinking positively to boost your confidence and courage in doing your work on hand.

Make your experience your stepping stone for success and Happiness without worrying about the harm in the future.

Make failure an opportunity to learn and improve your knowledge, skills, and abilities. One needs to learn to accept the outcomes in the present, bear the pain due to something not happening in the present and look forward to providing better performance in the future by not repeating the mistakes already done.

Failure on its own does not destroy our Happiness. Our Happiness is destroyed due to our negative reaction to any activity on hand. Fear can easily be overcome by properly training your mind for every action.

Once you learn the art of mastering fear, then the fear of failure will motivate you to improve. Other people will trust you more and your productivity will increase due to 100% concentration on your work on hand. You will be able to achieve results as per your goals and you will make yourself and others happy.

Weapon to destroy the Fear: Reframe the fearful thoughts and focus on your activity which you can perform with your knowledge, skills and abilities

4.Anger

What is Anger?

Anger is also known by other names, such a rage, and wrath.

Anger is created due to some trigger, but the reaction is based on the individual's ability to analyze the situation and react or respond to it.

For e.g., you are stuck in traffic. This event can act as a trigger for anger.

A happy person will analyze the situation and understand that the situation is not in his/her control.

He / She, rather than letting a negative emotion creep in, shall do a positive act like listening to his favorite music, watching an interesting movie, or even reading a humorous picture book.

Buddha reminds us that if we hold anger (like hot coal) for blasting it at someone, we are the one who gets burned.

The main cause of anger is the non-fulfillment of desires. We get angry when the outcomes do not meet our expectations.

Shri Krishna in Bhagavad Gita has stated that anger is the greatest enemy of human beings and, of course, happiness.

Anger originates from our big list of desires and higher self-esteem or ego, making us believe that we are capable of getting anything.

This inflated ego dilutes our memory about our real capabilities.

The moment we don't get the outcomes as per our expectations, the inflated ego even goes ahead to dilute our intellect.

We are not able to understand that our outcomes are based on the inputs. And at this state, a violent reaction comes out of us in the form of anger, which ultimately culminates in the destruction of happiness.

Any activity that is done by a disturbed, agitated and angry mind always leads to failure and harmful effects.

Research suggests that anger can arise due to certain habits and attitudes such as a high sense of ego, high attachment to external objects, non-satisfaction with what one has, discontented mind wanting to have more than adequate, using emotions to control the environment, refusal to listen to others point of views, lower tolerance for others views, criticizing and blaming others for your faults or mismatch between expectations and actual outcomes.

Deterioration of health

The first harmful effect of anger is the deterioration of health due to the release of stress hormones. If anger becomes a habit for every action, then it can destroy the neurons in the brain and eventually weaken your memory and immune system.

Just like fear, anger is also a basic emotion essential for the survival and wellbeing of a human being. Anger should be used to fight a challenging situation rather than fleeing from the harmful effects of blaming others for not getting the things you want.

If a person is able to justify his / her anger for bringing in some good change, then it won't be considered an outrage. In fact, it would increase the happiness of the person as well as others who are involved in the act.

However, any anger which results in frustration or sometimes even into activities to do physical harm to others will always result in the downfall of the person and make him / her unhappy in life.

Mindful Meditation

The first step to overcome anger is to take a deep breath and analyze the consequence of destructive anger.

Once you take a deep breath, start meditating on the Higher Self.

Make positive affirmations. "I have observed the signs of anger in me due to a particular event. I know this anger has no justification, and it can cause serious harm to me. I am replacing these angry thoughts with positive thoughts of compassion, love, and contentment. I am now doing my next action with a cool mind."

Do your best with a cool mind.

Once you make this affirmation, focus on the best action you can take under that situation.

You cannot avoid a situation, but you can certainly respond to it with a careful analysis and devising the best possible response.

Identify the root cause of anger and distance yourself from the root cause of anger.

If you carefully notice the events that are happening in your life, there will be many situations or circumstances repeatedly causing anger to you.

Identify the root causes of such anger and distance yourself from the root cause of anger so that you do not leverage the trigger of anger. For e.g., if meeting with a certain person makes you angry, then unless it is essential avoid the meeting.

However, in the home or at the workplace, we cannot avoid such anger-causing triggers. In such cases, the best way to control anger is to focus on your work and ignore the things you don't like about another person.

Remember, I have already said, the harmful effects of anger do not come from the trigger but from the reaction or response we provide to the trigger.

Happiness is your choice, and hence if you want to be happy, you need to master this art of responding to anger rather than reacting to the trigger of anger.

Never hold a grudge:

Learn the art to forgive and let go of the negative emotions created due to the harm provided by others or their contributions not coming as per your expectations.

Forgiveness will preserve your energy, and you will be able to spot the best response to create a win-win situation for you as well as others.

Express your anger

Some people have a unique way of expressing their anger. Rather than showing a violent reaction, they will make a loud count of numbers 1 to 10 in the reverse order, or write their anger on a piece of paper and tear it out, make a small drawing or painting to shift their angry mood into the art, listen to favorite music, give a mighty laugh in an angry situation to bring down the angry hormones, do some stretching or even take a time out and discuss the problem with a friend.

Use humor to puncture the tension in the environment

A hot atmosphere created by anger can burn everyone. An angry person can make use of humor as a fire extinguisher by punching humor, even in angry situations. Humor can lighten up the environment and bring in cooperation from all.

Seek help if your anger is not controllable

If your anger is not controllable seek help from professionals such as happiness coaches, psychologists, etc., for overcoming negative emotions such as fear, anger, etc.

Professionals can help you with some relaxation exercises and therapies that reduce or even eliminate your anger.

<u>Weapon to destroy Anger</u>:   Forgive others for their misdeeds and let go of the negative emotions. Practice gratitude and thank God for what he has given and get going with the situation.

What is Greed?

Greed is also an emotion that creates an intense desire to achieve something.

Greed drives us to an obsessive pursuit of accumulating more of everything we desire.

A person may be greedy to acquire power, wealth, ambition, name, fame, etc.

The biggest reason for Greed is lack of contentment. Greed triggers from a desire to have something more, irrespective of whether you have that something inadequate or not.

Greedy people create a big void in their inner mind, and hence they always focus their time, energy, and efforts on gathering more things for e.g., some people are so crazy at accumulating huge wealth that they are willing to compromise their family life, relationships, the welfare of their dependent children, etc.

Greedy people have a big ambition for material gains and success in accumulating huge possessions.

Mahatma Gandhi has made a very important observation on Greed,

"The world has enough for everyone's need, but not enough for everyone's greed."

- Mahatma Gandhi

Gandhiji clearly points out the real source of Greed is discontentment. The endless chase towards endless material gains or pleasure transforms a happy mind into an unhappy mind when all the things that are desired are not accumulated.

Yes, material comforts can relieve you from the emotional discomfort of not having something. But a happy person always practices altruism, i.e., keeping the essential for self and giving away other possessions for the well-being of other people.

The best examples of non-greedy but happy people are philanthropists such as Jamshedji Tata, Bill and Melinda Gates, Henry Wellcome, Warren Buffett, Mukesh Ambani, Azim Premji, Shiv Nadar, Kumar Mangalam Birla, Anil Agrawal, etc.

A small amount of Greed is essential for motivating oneself for social welfare and not for social unrest.

The destructing factor in Greed is the lust for amassing more and more possessions for self rather than the welfare of the society.

Unchecked Greed can bring the downfall of society and the destruction of a human being.

Sooner or later, a time will come when the human being will realize that he has accumulated too much on things really not required by him and has wasted his life on accumulating possessions rather than meeting his ultimate goal in life, i.e., happiness.

Greedy people need to be committed, have patience, be persistent, be humble and show courage to please the inner self rather than seek gratification and validations from the outer world.

One should aim for getting only that part that one really needs. Only then will the person have time, energy, and effort for realizing the real self and being happy.

If Greed is not controlled, then a small desire to acquire more can turn into an uncontrolled longing for having more, in spite of having sufficient and adequate material.

Some people describe Greed as a sin after considering the devastating effects created by Greed.

Greed gives rise to other negative emotions such as selfishness, anger, comparison, jealousy, unfair competition, stress, anxiety, depression, exhaustion, and despair that sucks happiness. Greed can lead to arrogance, callousness, megalomania, and totally destroy empathy towards others.

Signs of Greed: self-centeredness, envy towards others, lack of empathy, manipulate others for personal gains, stressed and anxious to gain more possession

Greed starts with a small desire to provide for the essentials of a human being and his family.

Greed indeed masquerades an essential desire in such cases.

However, it does not take much time to convert such essential desires into non-essential desires, knowingly or unknowingly, when a human being simply focuses on accumulating possessions for showing them off rather than for routine essentials and comforts.

This dangerous act of Greediness totally destroys the inner consciousness of the person, and he forgets the real purpose of life.

Such a person becomes restless and losses peace of mind and happiness. In his pursuit of accumulating more possessions, he may also get involved in illegal acts and someday get punished for the crimes committed by him/her.

One of the most destructive effects of Greed is that it drives you away from the real source of Joy, i.e., the Higher Self.

If you believe in your Higher Self, you will be sure that you are going to get the right essentials at the right time.

You don't have to waste your life accumulating huge possessions. Instead, you should focus on converting your craving into contentment and grumbling into gratitude.

A Greedy person wants more and is never satisfied with what he/she has.

He keeps on eating the junk food available at different corners of the food street.

Such a person forgets the delicious taste of his favorite homemade food. Instead of relishing on-time-tested home food, a greedy person wants to taste as many varieties of the food as possible.

Ultimately, he/she spoils his appetite, hunger, health, and there is a danger of some variety of food causing harm to the internal body organs, including the stomach, lungs, intestines, brain, and mind.

A greedy person will always have conflicts and arguments with his near and dear ones, and hence Greed can ruin the relationships.

Such a conflict and arguments can arise when you start manipulating others for fulfilling your desires.

Focus on acquiring the real wealth

If at all you want to be greedy, have your Greediness to accumulate more blessings from God. The practice of gratitude, contentment, and generosity can easily secure more blessings, and such accumulations will never destroy your happiness. In fact, you will be the owner of long-lasting happiness.

Practice Gratitude and Contentment

Practice the attitude of gratitude and contentment, which is the number 1 antidote for Greed. Focus on what you have and enjoy it.

If the need increases, get that too but don't steal others possession for increasing your gains

Understand your role in life

When we understand the role given to us in this life by God, we will not run after accumulating possessions.

We will strive to get what is essential and reject the Greed of gathering more than that is essential.

By doing this, our mind will be focused on the right action, and we can enjoy the results with tranquility rather than over striving and toil.

Don't fall on the slippery slope of Greed

Stay away from temptations and instant gratifications, which will force you to find different ways of acquiring them.

Show the exit doors to the foolish and harmful desires which can ruin total happiness. Embrace the upstream slope of Contentment, Satisfaction, and Gratitude instead of slippery slope of Greed.

Be Generous

Our scriptures state that whatever we get belongs to the Universe.

We have temporary possession of the things under our control.

We are simply the trustees of it and use the things for our essential requirements and give them back to the Universe by distributing them to the needy.

 If you do such a kind act, you will manifest Generosity and an important antidote to Greediness.

None stops you from acquiring possessions honestly, but you should not entertain the act of Greed that forces you to steal and keep what belongs to others.

When Greed takes the front seat to drive your car, you will surely not reach your main destination, but your car will be tossing and turning in different unending directions.

Ultimately this tipsy topsy driving will take you away from your main goal and destroy the happiness of life. Be safe with your driving, and let not Greed creep in your driver.

Weapon to destroy Greed: Live a minimalist life full of contentment, satisfaction, gratitude, generosity and acquire your essentials rather than running after non-essential things

Conclusion

I have spoken in detail about the five worst enemies of happiness in this chapter.

I can give more details about most of the enemies of happiness in my three days Happiness Blueprint workshops.

You may let me know if you are interested to discover the enemies of happiness and conquering them all.

We experience ruthless attacks from these enemies of happiness. We don't realize them then, as our vision is clouded with unhappiness, and our brain is under the total control of our lower self.

We could find a vaccine for the devastating Coronavirus, but very few happiness scientists are working on a vaccine to protect us from this unhappiness epidemic. We desperately seek help without investigating the root causes of these enemies of happiness.

Now you are equipped with fighting battles with the main enemies of happiness and destroying them to enjoy long-lasting happiness.

Use these weapons right now and make this world a better place to live and help others too.

✓ We should prioritize listing all these causes of disturbance of peace and happiness and call them enemies of happiness. Once we make a list of happiness enemies, we should attack them one at a time so that our focus becomes very strong against these enemies. Since we attack them one at a time, each enemy becomes the No. 1 enemy for that moment of attack.

✓ Five worst enemies of happiness:
1. Jumping Mind 2. Ego 3. Fear 4. Anger 5. Greed.

✓ Weapon to destroy the Jumping Mind: Transform your Jumping Mind to Mindful Mind.

✓ Weapon to destroy the Self-centred Ego: Transform the Self-centred Ego to Self-less Ego.

✓ Weapon to destroy the Fear: Reframe the fearful thoughts and focus on your activity which you can perform with your knowledge, skills and abilities.

✓ Weapon to destroy Anger: Forgive others for their misdeeds and let go of the negative emotions. Practice gratitude and thank God for what he has given and get going with the situation.

✓ Weapon to destroy Greed: Live a minimalist life full of contentment, satisfaction, gratitude, generosity and acquire your essentials rather than running after non-essential things.

Chapter 5: Simple lies about Happiness

A little boy asked a little girl, "Are you happy?"

The little girl replied, "Yes, I am happy because I have many cute dolls to play with."

A teacher asked an MBA graduate on the convocation day, "Since you have topped your batch, Are you happy?"

The MBA graduate replied, "I will be happy when I get a good job with a good salary."

A crow and white pigeon were flying together in the open sky. The crow asked the pigeon, "Are you happy?"

The pigeon replied, "Yes, I am happy, but I would have been happier if I could change my body color from white to black."

A young girl was stuck in grief because she could not get a much-awaited promotion and a hike in salary. Her colleague suggested that she work hard and rise in the next turn. The young girl disagreed with her colleagues and believed that she won't get her promotion and will never be happy in life.

Many people and living beings try to find happiness at things, events, and circumstances, but true happiness is unavailable in any of them.

Research has revealed that true happiness lies in the way we look and think and hence is within us and not within things, events, and circumstances.

In our happiness journey, it is imperative to segregate the simple lies about happiness from the simple truths about happiness.

Let us understand simple lies about happiness in this chapter, and in the next chapter, we will speak about simple truths about happiness.

Simple lies about happiness can also be called Myths about Happiness. Myths are beliefs made by people and established over a while. Since happiness depends upon people's perception, someday, someone may find a deeper meaning and discover the falsity of the myth.

Some myths about happiness may give us a wrong notion of becoming happy, while other tales may make us feel miserable. There can be no magic formula for happiness nor a sure-fire course to remove unhappiness.

Hence it is essential to understand the meaning behind the myths and blend their usefulness with our journey of true happiness.

Here are the collections of my favorite myths about happiness:

Yes, we are born with a happy state of mind and are naturally happy. As we grow, our mind is conditioned or programmed with many learnings.

These learnings put us in a survival mode, and we start feeling scarcity in life.

As we move to fill the void, we may achieve success and occasional failures.

Our so-called natural happy mind gets the jerks of ups and downs, success and failures in life.

In this situation, it is entirely our choice to remain happy with a positive response to every type of outcome-whether good or bad.

Hence, even though happiness is naturally available we need to work for creating our happiness.

2. Happiness depends upon success in achieving material gains

Happiness does not literally depend upon success in achieving material gains. Happiness purely depends upon contentment and satisfaction with whatever we have.

Remember we read the story of the fisherman and the business tycoon in chapter number three.

Yes, momentary gains will give you pleasure and comfort, but true happiness does not depend entirely on material gains.

In fact, the more you acquire possession, the higher will be the responsibility and stress to manage and maintain it.

Happiness does not really depend on material gains but on satisfaction and contentment.

We must learn to accept what nature has given to us and work towards the role assigned by nature to each one of us. We will automatically get what is meant for us.

3. Happiness is a destination and not a journey

Most people spend their life in accumulating wealth to enjoy in the future.

These people feel that if the resources are consumed now, they won't have enough resources left for the future.

Well, one cannot compromise on being happy now and simply stocking everything for the future.

Who knows, you may not survive to enjoy your accumulated possessions in the future.

Your accumulations may fall into the wrong hands of people who don't have a value for your hard-earned accumulations.

Well, you don't have to consume everything now, but do not starve for it for enjoying in the future.

Happiness is a journey with small destinations.

Hence after every milestone, you should celebrate and enjoy making your entire journey filled with long-lasting happiness.

4. Children are happier than grown-ups and elders

Each stage of life is different, and it purely depends upon us how we seek happiness in our pursuit of happiness.

It is a wrong notion to think that children are happier than grown-ups and elders.

Children have a very tender mind, and their happiness depends upon very few things.

As we grow, we come across various new desires, and our mind runs after essential and non-essential desires.

We have to give priority to which desires to choose for sustaining our happiness.

Just because we obtain new knowledge, skills, and money power, if we fall prey to endless desires, then one cannot be happy.

In fact, elderly people are supposed to be happier as they have calmed down in life, have fewer desires, and savor their happy moments in life.

Hence happiness is available for all ages. We can teach our children to be happy and also remember the same art and science of happiness to enjoy a happy life.

5. Happiness comes by luck and chance

If happiness had come by luck or chance, no person on the earth would have worked towards making life meaningful, and fulfilled.

We need to strive and thrive to become happy.

Happiness is our choice, and we need to learn the art and science of becoming happy in all situations and circumstances.

You can have a positive affirmation to wish what you desire or you can even generate positive vibrations for letting your things happen. It's up to the Universe to give it to you.

But that does not mean you need not work to create your own happiness.

Well, if something good comes your way during this process, it is welcome.

Just because you got something by chance or luck, it cannot be concluded that the entire happiness comes by luck and chance.

6. Happiness comes from external material pleasures

If children like toys, then their happiness should always come from toys, but it is not so.

If a person gets all comfort materials right from a house, car, good job, latest electronic gadgets, etc., then his / her happiness should always come from such external sources, but it is not so.

Research has revealed that the more you have of something, the lesser the satisfaction comes in later utilization of the same resources.

Yes, these external sources generate the happiness hormones for the time being, but we have seen so many rich people claiming they are not happy with it.

On the other hand, we have also seen many poor people without having sufficient external resources to enjoy life, claiming that they are happy.

So, happiness does not necessarily come from external material pleasures.

7. Happiness is outside in rather than inside out

In the above myth, we have seen that happiness is not dependent on external sources.

We have also seen that poor people, with limited resources, can thoroughly enjoy their life.

Happiness is an emotion that can be created within us without the help of external resources.

Hence happiness is not outside in but an inside out phenomenon.

The feeling of contentment, satisfaction, and gratitude will help us to experience happiness inside out.

8. A simple and minimalist life won't create happiness in life

The more complicated your life is, the more is the confusion.

Conversely, the more simplistic and minimalist life you live, the clearer your mind is to enjoy happiness every moment.

In our previous myths, we have seen that happiness does not depend on our possessions and accumulation.

What we need are the basic essentials.

If we look at our life minutely, we will notice that we have been brought into this world by the creator.

Our daily needs and essentials are also taken care of by the creators.

What is really required are our efforts as per the role given to us.

However, if one goes beyond the role prescribed by the Universe, then life becomes complicated, and we unknowingly fall into the unhappiness trap.

A simple and minimalist life will provide peace of mind, less stress, and happiness every moment.

9.Your job or business will make you happy

Whether you are a salaried person or an entrepreneur, you cannot firmly say that your job or business will make you happy.

Before a couple of decades, there was a common belief that when people join an organization, they retire in the same organization.

Similarly, the entrepreneur would pass on his/her business skills to the next generation and will take voluntary retirement at his older age.

In the twenty-first century, especially after the Covid pandemic, jobs and businesses have become uncertain.

Even though you are in your job or business, there is no certainty how long you will remain in the same job or business.

The need of the hour is to balance your work and life and at the same time upskill and upgrade so that you can adapt to any change in the environment.

If you get stuck on one job or business, a sudden change may land up in you losing the job or closure of business.

Hence happiness is not in your job or business but in your adaptation to the situations and circumstances of life.

10.Happiness can be obtained with loneliness

Loneliness is a disease, and it cannot give birth to a positive emotion like happiness.

Yes, you can experience a calm and serene mind when you are alone, but human being is a social animal and requires the company to enjoy a fulfilled life.

Here comes the need for generosity, as all human beings are not equal.

When you break your loneliness, you learn to share both good and bad things with others and enjoy happiness.

It is believed that extroverts are happier than introverts due to openness and participation in social networks.

Loneliness may create stress and anxiety as you may not share your ups and downs in life.

Only when you release your stress hormones will you get full peace of mind.

A peaceful mind can lead to happiness rather than a lonely mind.

11.Surrender to nature and accept everything to become happy

Acceptance is the topmost remedy to prevent a mind from agitations and disturbances. Every person has the freedom to act.

Our actions can be planned to improve our life. Acceptance does not mean only surrendering to nature and not putting in any efforts to improve life.

Acceptance is followed by learning and improving from our mistakes by putting in the best efforts in our next attempt.

Putting efforts is in our hands.

The outcomes are to be accepted as a gift from God.

There is no point in grumbling about the outcomes, but one should certainly put more attention on planning and implementing its efforts for enjoying happiness in every action.

So, acceptance does not mean blind acceptance but mindful acceptance.

12. We are not happy because of someone else's fault

Our happiness cannot depend on doing or not doing something by someone else. Every human being is responsible as well as accountable for their actions. If one develops the attitude of responsibility accounting, it can improve and increase the chances of success and happiness.

One should not criticize, blame or point fingers at others for failures and unhappiness. Instead of criticizing, blaming, or pointing fingers at others, one should identify the root cause of failure and unhappiness and put in efforts to destroy the root cause of failure and unhappiness.

Conclusion

I have made an attempt to provide you with a clear view of myths of happiness. This is the right time to bust the myths of happiness and find real happiness.

We are responsible for breaking the false promises made to us relating to making us happy. Well, I agree that there may be another side to the myths.

Those who made such myths had their purpose and plan behind it. But it may hold good only in a particular situation or circumstance. These myths cannot be considered as universal truths of happiness. My earnest request to my reader is to understand the deeper meaning behind the myths and try to understand whether it fits in your life. Else, go for the universal truths of happiness.

- ✓ Simple lies about happiness can also be called Myths about Happiness. Myths are beliefs made by people and established over a while.
- ✓ Happiness depends upon people's perception, someday, someone may find a deeper meaning and discover the falsity of the myth.
- ✓ Some myths about happiness may give us a wrong notion of becoming happy, while other tales may make us feel miserable.
- ✓ It is essential to understand the meaning behind the myths and blend their usefulness with our journey of true happiness.
- ✓ Myth number 1: Happiness is naturally available for human beings.
- ✓ Myth number 2: Happiness depends upon success in achieving material gains.
- ✓ Myth number 3: Happiness is a destination and not a journey.

- ✓ Myth number 4: Children are happier than grown-ups and elders.
- ✓ Myth number 5: Happiness comes by luck and chance.
- ✓ Myth number 6: Happiness comes from external material pleasures.
- ✓ Myth number 7: Happiness is outside in rather than inside out.
- ✓ Myth number 8: A simple and minimalist life won't create happiness in life.
- ✓ Myth number 9: Your job or business will make you happy.
- ✓ Myth number 10: Happiness can be obtained with loneliness.
- ✓ Myth number 11: Surrender to nature and accept everything to become happy.
- ✓ Myth number 12: We are not happy because of someone else's fault.

Chapter 6: Simple truths about Happiness

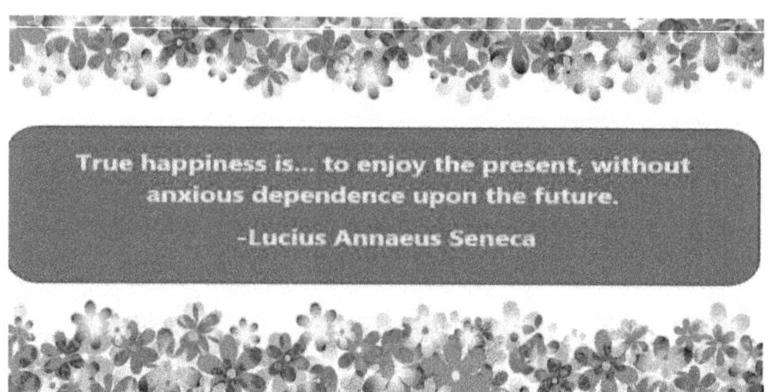

In the previous chapter, we understood the need for knowing and busting the myths about happiness to arrive at the true meaning of happiness.

In this chapter, we will look at simple truths about happiness.

Knowing the Truth about happiness is also important before we begin our journey to learn how to be happy under all circumstances and situations.

Modern society is conditioned with a different meaning of happiness. A new seeker of happiness is not able to understand the Truth and Lies behind happiness.

Some believe that happiness can be bought with money, while others believe happiness depends on the materials available for enjoyment.

When one looks at reality, one finds that some people are unhappy all the time, in spite of having everything they desire, while others are happy all the time in spite of not having sufficient things to survive.

Hence it is essential to know some simple truths about happiness in the crazy and highly developed world of the twenty-first century.

Secret truths about happiness

Let me list out some of the secret truths about happiness.

1. True Happiness can be experienced in both pleasure and pain

Happiness without pleasure seems to be an absurd statement.

True Happiness can be experienced in both pleasure and pain.

For example, a person will get pleasure after buying a new car of his own.

Similarly, a mother, in spite of the tremendous labor pain while giving birth to a child, is also happy to get the first glimpses of the newborn child.

Relief from pain also helps to increase happiness levels.

Pleasure and Pain are the part and parcel of life for every human being. Many people consider pain as an essential resource for Happiness rather than a signal of failure in not getting what one has desired.

Some people have a wrong notion of Happiness. Such people feel that one will be happy all the time, 365 days, 24x7.

Both good things and bad things are experienced by happy people. But since they know how to deal with bad and sad things, their response is controlled, which in turn reduces the impact of the bad and sad things.

Happy people are determined to remain happy under all situations and circumstances.

However, our complete Happiness will depend on experiencing pain and learning to cope with positive emotions.

One should not jump to grim conclusions and go into a bad mood after experiencing pain and hurt.

Happy people master the grit and resiliency skills to bounce back from any lows experienced in life.

One of the best examples of creating Happiness out of pain is the delivery of a sad song enveloped with sad emotions. The singer puts in his heart and soul while singing a sad song as he is undergoing the pain.

However, he is very happy to produce a good quality song album.

Getting habituated to deal with pains in an effective manner helps us to face challenges in life with resilience and remain happy in all situations and circumstances.

2. Happiness is a choice based on our perspective

Happiness is indeed a choice we have to make every day, right from birth to death.

Some people feel that they can be happy due to luck or chance. But that's not true.

Based on the situations and circumstances, one has to decide to entertain certain thoughts.

Based on one's thoughts, one can get the feeling of acting in a particular way.

If our actions are performed with positive emotions, we experience happiness in the outcome of the actions.

Once you make the right choice and put positive emotions into your work, you can certainly enjoy a happy life consciously.

When one's decided to choose happiness, one's life gets a meaning and purpose, and all actions are focused on creating happiness in every effort.

The results will make one glad and jubilant and inspire you to live a life with hope and optimism.

When one makes happiness a choice, one's thoughts, words, and actions should be in harmony, and hence one might have to build good habits and develop a positive mindset

Even in sad circumstances and failures, one can choose to be happy.

The best way to choose happiness in sad times is to think about the happy moments in life and apply the reasons one is happy now.

One may not recreate a lost thing or regret on broken relationship, but one can certainly live a happy life by enjoying the present moment with peace of mind, confidence, and excitement.

Happiness does not happen overnight. Develop the art of happiness by noting minute details of what makes you happy, and use them in times of need.

3. Self-Awareness can lead to Happiness

Self-Awareness involves knowing about one's character, feelings, desires, and goals of life.

Self-Awareness helps an individual to focus and objectively evaluate whether one's thoughts, emotions, and actions are aligned with their chosen path of Happiness.

Every person has a Higher Self and lower self-hidden within itself.

The Higher Self always guides a person to do all things that leads to Happiness.

The lower self generally leads to unhappiness.

So, if the person is aware of the Higher Self, then he/she can easily objectively evaluate whether his/her thoughts, emotions, and actions are aligned with one's chosen path of Happiness.

If there is a mismatch, then corrections can happen every moment so that the person can enjoy Happiness every moment.

In addition to being aware of the virtues of the Higher Self, every person should also be aware of the social norms so that one is very clear to perform one's role in a manner acceptable to society.

Self-Awareness helps us to build an ability to check our actions and recognize their impact on others.

We get more clarity in dealing with people based on our strengths and make better decisions based on multiple perspectives.

4. Happiness increases by giving happiness to others

Happiness is like a kiss. You must share it to enjoy it."

-Bernard Meltzer

Research has revealed that happiness increases by sharing anything you like with others. For e.g., a smile provides joy to you, and when others see your smile, they also respond with a smile that makes you happier.

In addition to making, you happy, a natural smile has powers to reduce stress, elevate mood, lower blood pressure, boost the immune system, and spread it in all directions.

Sharing ignites three main positive emotions within us: Empathy, Compassion, and Altruism.

Empathy helps us to experience the feelings, thoughts and experience both positive and negative emotions of others.

Empathy can be manifested at the mind level and emotional level. At the mind level, you enter into the minds of others and think the way they think. Once you clone their mind, you also experience the feelings of other persons.

When one experienced the feelings of another person, one shows emotional empathy. When one experiences the functioning of the mind of another person, one shows cognitive empathy. When one does some activities to help the other person based on emotional and cognitive empathy, one shows compassionate empathy.

When we were small babies, our mother taught us empathy skills. For e.g., our mother smiled when we smiled, and coincidentally the baby in us also smiled when the mother smiled. I hope you are able to relate with me.

What does this smile strategy teach us?

This smiling strategy teaches us to express how we feel, and the mother also replicates the same feeling to establish a strong bonding between the child and the mother.

Impact of a smile:

When you flash a hearty smile, all your 72 face muscles are involved in directing your brain to manufacture happiness hormones.

The happiness hormones change your unhappy mood to a happy mood by eliminating stress, if any.

That's not all! Your happy mood infects others and makes them happy, too, as a smile is contagious. Smiles spread positive vibrations and manifest a good part of life.

Once you develop the habit of smiling, you start living a healthy life. A healthy life boosts your immune system and increases your longevity. Intense smiling can help you live a long and happy life.

When you smile even in negative and unfavorable circumstances, your smiling response reduces the pain and hurt.

One looks more attractive because of one's smile, as God has gifted everyone a unique smile.

One can succeed in one's life by using a smile as the biggest weapon to prepare one's mood to meet different challenges and situations of life.

Research has revealed that small babies ignored by their parents have very disturbing adulthood and thus fail to enjoy happiness.

Empathy puts an important focus on relationships and improves our connection with others for enjoying happiness. Being social animals, we are created in a way to share our experiences with others in order to become happy. If we don't have a companion to share our happiness with, we won't be able to broadcast our happiness.

Empathy can be useful in both happy and sad situations. When someone shares good news, we celebrate the good things with others.

When there is sad news, one understands the sad feelings of others and try to console the person so that the pain or hurt is reduced.

By showing empathy in sad situations, one can help others from exhibiting violent, impulsive reactions to negative interpretations. Empathy showers should show sympathy but should not get infected with the sadness of others.

It is true that one's happiness is not dependent on any external factors. But what we are talking about is to live a happy life in a social environment wherein we are surrounded by other people-some of them known to us, while others can be strangers.

When we are on an assignment, we have to relocate our living place or even have to travel with strangers. Hence this art of empathy can be useful in all situations.

Our empathy skills can be improved by carefully observing others and paying attention to both verbal and nonverbal communication.

Compassion: In addition to showing empathy, compassion imparts a desire to help others to come out of hardships and distress.

It diverts your attention from looking at yourself to looking at others' problems with an intention to help them to solve their problem.

Even though you help others, your happiness increases more than others who have actually solved their problems.

One big benefit of Compassion is that it helps you to think beyond yourself, which is an important aspect of creating happiness.

Compassion leads to **Altruism** by generating a kind and selfless behavior to help others.

Right from childhood, children are encouraged to share their things, howsoever dear to them, with other children.

The idea over here is to stop children from developing the habit of selfishness and develop Compassion for kids who cannot afford or have such things.

The children are already happy to own their possessions, but when they share them with others, their happiness is multiplied.

As we grow with age, somehow, we get attached to personal belongings and forget the golden habit inculcated from our childhood.

One has to revive this habit to increase one's happiness levels. This habit also establishes and improves relationships.

In a joint family system, the entire house is shared by all the family members.

No one cribs for sharing but all stay happily in spite of the house and other belongings being shared by the family members.

Parents tell bedtime moral stories to a small kid. I would suggest, all of us can share our happiness stories with each other, irrespective of the age barrier.

Your happiness story can inspire others to tell their own stories of happiness.

Do you remember when you have helped someone to come out of distress or have manifested kindness and generosity with random act of kindness to help an old person cross the pedestrian zebra crossing?

Remember, Compassion does not come after another person asking for help.

It is your proactiveness to feel the hardships of other people and a sincere desire to help them face the hardship easily and come out of it.

One big advantage of showing Compassion is projecting your image as a superhero in the eyes of others for the help provided by you to come out of hardship and sadness.

Above all, Compassion gives you a sense of satisfaction and fulfillment in life. It can enhance your health, well-being, and longevity as well.

5. Everyone can be happy at all times
Happiness is the topmost goal of everyone.

Every human being strives to become happy and, in this process, also the envy of others who are already happy.

Most people try to excel in personal achievements and experience happiness in showing off their possessions to others for claiming their happiness.

Let me warn you here. Happiness is not meant for a few people, but it is the birth right of all human beings.

Just imagine you are watching an IPL cricket T20 match where the world's top players are pitted against each other through different franchise teams.

Even though no national side is playing against any national side, the moment the boundaries and sixers are hit, or a bowler takes a wicket or a fielder dive to take an excellent catch, all the spectators in the stadium erupt into happiness.

They all enjoy happiness through the medium of cricket. It does not matter which player belongs to which country.

Similarly, every human being can be happy in this big stadium of life.

We are all the players in it. Just like any player can hit a four or a six or can take a wicket and do excellent fielding, we too can do our role and be happy and make others happy too.

One should make a careful note that everyone can be happy all the time if one performs their role with positive emotions.

Such an act can make this world a better place to live in and everyone can enjoy happiness not only for oneself but for all the human beings on this Earth.

Happiness can be increased by living in an environment that supports happiness.

Supportive people can play a big role by showing love, empathy, and compassion, which can culminate into boosting one's confidence and eventually create happiness for oneself and others.

True happiness can be created by accepting our self for doing our best and accepting others as they are.

Some common things that can make everyone happy:

Wake up refreshed: Learn to get a good 8 hours sleep and wake up refreshed in the morning.

Give love to get love: A loving partner (can be your spouse, children, friend, or even a stranger) can boost your happiness.

Keep fit: Stay active by proactive exercise in whatever way appeals to you.

Have goals: Have lots of small goals and celebrate achieving each one

Build a happiness nest : Build a happiness nest to unwind your retreat: It can be in your house, your bedroom, or even the bathroom.

Pace yourself: Make the best use of time for performing your activities rather than chasing time to manage them. This habit will help you become productive without loading yourself with heavy work.

Celebrate your success with treats: Share your joy with your near and dear ones with appropriate treats. No one will refuse a treat. When you reward yourself with a treat, you will remain self-motivated for further success in your life.

Give gifts with an open heart: Giving gifts to others reminds you that what you have got from others needs to be shared with others for increasing your prosperity with getting more in the future.

When you make others happy by giving them gifts, their happiness further increases your happiness.

Tolerant attitude: Never get infected with the illness of others. Instead, be a doctor and treat them. Their illness can be a sad mind, an angry mind, a vengeance mind, a mind full of greed and lust, etc.

Learn to tolerate the pain, hurt, and critic hurled upon you and simultaneously treat them as an illness. You can cure their illness with sympathy, empathy, and compassion.

Play like a kid irrespective of your age: Playing any game creates a flow, and we get absorbed in an activity. One can also engage into activities they like such as drawing, painting, dancing, singing, cooking etc. It generates a similar outcome as meditation.

The only difference is we sit for a meditation whereas we involve ourselves with others while playing. The best part of playing is you can play with anyone, for e.g., your spouse, children, friends, and even strangers, both online as well as offline.

6. Happier people succeed in life, but successful people may not be happy

Shawn Achor, the famous author of The Happiness Advantage, states that happiness leads to tremendous success in the TEDx talk.

Some people believe that they will be happy if they succeed in life. However, that is not so.

Research has revealed that happy people tend to be successful in life, family, workplace, relationships, etc.

7. Happiness can be found by connecting with nature

Most human beings are fond of being in the lap of nature. As soon as one gets an opportunity, a visit to a hill station, beach, snowy mountain is planned to enjoy the beauty of nature.

Nature's scene can have a tremendous impact on human beings. It can reduce anger, fear, and stress and increase positive emotions.

Regular visits to naturally beautiful places can gift a person with healthy life and wellbeing. A calm mind will also increase productivity and happiness.

Some people make a habit of going for a morning walk to be with nature in a noise-less environment, while others prefer to grow small plants in their house.

Nature has the capability to soothe us and refresh our minds to accept and face any challenges in life.

8. Good relationships can make you happy

People who love themselves are in a better position to love others. Loving others results in friendship. Friendship leads to sharing of feelings (both happy and sad). Sharing feelings releases happiness hormones and reduces stress hormones.

When one listens to one's partner carefully and responds proactively, it deepens their relationships and lays a solid foundation for enjoying happiness for a longer duration.

Well, one should be alert when attachments create feelings of negative emotions such as jealousy and not positive emotions such as euphoria and excitement.

One should learn to value other people's happiness as much as its own.

Infatuation can generate an intense feeling of attraction without any sense of commitment. However, if you are serious about your relationship, even infatuation can be converted into lasting love.

Compassionate love helps to build trust, affection, and commitment as well.

There is no single rule for love and friendship as every person is different. However, if you follow the basic rules of happiness, your friendship can easily blossom into a longer-lasting happy relationship.

9. Happy people consciously use positive thoughts by identifying with the Higher Self
Happy people consciously use positive thoughts by identifying with the Higher Self.

Every human being is surrounded by both positive and negative thoughts. However, instead of identifying with the lower self, happy people always surrender to their

Higher Self and close all entry points for the lower self.

Yes, the lower self will play its role to surround you with negative thoughts, but if happiness is the choice you want to make, then you will always identify with the Higher Self and give birth to positive thoughts, feelings, actions, and results. By doing this, you will always remain happy

10. Happiness is experienced while working towards the goal

Some people believe that they will enjoy Happiness after reaching a goal. In this process, they postpone the enjoyment of Happiness. When they start enjoying Happiness after reaching their goal, their happy moments vanish. Time and Happiness wait for no one.

Happy moments are to be enjoyed as and when they come. This process of enjoying Happiness in the present moment makes the life journey full of joy and satisfaction without anger, stress, and anxiety.

A wise person uses his intelligence to make important decisions in life. A wise person lives a relaxed life and is guided by nature as to what to do and what not to do.

A wise person learns to be happy with himself/herself and focuses on basic needs rather than unwanted needs and desires.

He/ She uses the intelligence to focus on essentials and do creative works for accomplishing goals of life.

A wise person is undisturbed by any disturbances or obstacles posed during their happiness journey.

A wise person is free from unwanted attachments and clings to compassion and gratitude while doing his/her daily activities.

A wise person is able to discriminate between right and wrong things and is always inspired and motivated to hold on to the right things.

12. A strong determination to be happy will always make you happy

Happiness is your birth right but comes in the invisible form with the soul. People who are determined to be happy have a strong willpower to be happy and don't blame others for their unhappiness.

Such people are aware of their inherent power of happiness, and they know the art of keeping away the distractions and disturbances causing unhappiness.

They are committed to being happy under all situations and circumstances.

Happiness is their priority. They know how to feed their happiness quotient to help it grow stronger.

Happy people don't wait for the circumstances to change. Instead, they make up their mind to remain happy every moment.

✓ True Happiness can be experienced in both pleasure and pain.
✓ Happiness is a choice based on our perspective.
✓ Self-Awareness can lead to Happiness.
✓ Happiness increases by giving happiness to others.
✓ Everyone can be happy at all times.
✓ Happier people succeed in life but successful people may not be happy.
✓ Happiness can be found by connecting with nature.
✓ Good relationships can make you happy.
✓ Happy people consciously use positive thoughts by identifying with the Higher Self.
✓ Happiness is experienced while working towards the goal.
✓ A wise man is spontaneously happy.
✓ A strong determination to be happy will always make you happy

Chapter 7: How to live a Happy life?

A short story to reflect on good virtues and wisdom

An old man was living with his son in a village. The son complains to the old man that he did not create any assets to leave behind after his death.

The old man asked his son, "Are you unhappy."

His son replied, "I cannot be unhappy at any moment."

The old man asked, "What is the secret of your happiness."

His son replied, "You have taught me throughout my life how to be happy in any situation and circumstance."

The old man's face lit up with pride, and he quickly reverted with an answer, "That's all you need for your remaining life."

His son realized his mistake and thanked his father for the precious wealth in the form of wisdom and virtues left by his old father for him.

The learning from this story is you cannot be happy in life by material pleasures. **The secret formula to happiness is to learn to live a happy life without even chasing to acquire more material possessions.**

In this chapter, we will learn the secret formula of living a happy life.

If you are the one who is wasting your life in unhappiness and Happiness is elusive for you, then this chapter will be very important to discover your Happiness.

If you want to become a Happiness Conqueror, you need to find the right address for Happiness.

As a human being evolves and the world is dominated by mechanized and automated business entities, your happiness skills and habits need to be fine-tuned to live a happy life in all situations and circumstance.

In order to succeed in this complex world, in addition to having a higher intelligence and emotional quotient, you also need to have a very good happiness quotient to succeed and thrive in this competitive world.

Both individuals and corporates have understood the importance of investing in improving the happiness quotient and spent their time, energy, and resources to master the art and science of Happiness.

It is believed that a lot many people are struggling to find total and long-lasting Happiness. Each one is trying to define their Happiness but is not able to find a sure-fire way of accomplishing Happiness and keep with it for a longer period.

If you go for a search of Happiness on Google, you will easily find "happiness" is one of the largely searched topics on the internet.

One big reason for this massive search for Happiness could be a lack of knowledge about where Happiness is and how to live a happy life.

Many people try to buy happiness with money, but money can only provide temporary comforts and pleasures, and it even reduces your miseries. Research states that money cannot provide Happiness as Happiness can be created and felt within every human being.

You don't have to search for Happiness in the external world, but Happiness exists in its natural state in your inner world.

You can easily discover your Happiness after becoming aware of yourself and living your life with a proper vision and goal.

I, too, was struggling to find the master keys of Happiness. I was frustrated to cope with the ups and downs in life and believed I could not be happy at all. However, with a focused approach and mindful thinking along with some useful skills and habits, I could conquer my enemies of Happiness.

After understanding what Happiness is, enemies of Happiness, simple lies, and truths about Happiness, we are perfectly geared to learn the skills, habits, secrets of living a happy life.

In this chapter, I will reveal all my secrets of Happiness which can be useful for children, teens, married people, single people, retired people, as well as those in their sunset years. These secrets of happiness are also useful at workplace to lead a productive, successful and happy life.

The basic steps of living a happy life would be the same, but some of the skills and habits can vary with age group.

Your Happiness depends entirely on your choice to be happy and the priority you give to your goal to be happy.

After we wake up and till the time we go to bed at night, we are surrounded by various obstacles that upset our happy life. The obstacles can be in the form of social media platforms, family matters, office matters, and even calls from friends. If we decide to be happy and give priority to living a happy life, we need to follow certain standards and best practices of Happiness.

Now I don't want to inject the fear of standards and best practices into your mind. We don't have to get certified with some ISO standards or best practices for living a happy life. But we certainly need to develop certain useful skills and habits.

All these skills and habits are to be developed based on one's experience in dealing with the enemies of Happiness. As I said before, I have over 30 years of exposure in the corporate world which includes dealing with all types of people across different geographies. I had to design my happiness skills and habits and use them to solve my happiness problems. The best part of these happiness skills and habits is their usefulness to different types of people in addition to me.

Hence, I strongly believe my happiness skills and habits can also be useful for many people. I have tried to include most of my happiness skills and habits in this chapter. I will talk more about it in detail in my **3 Days Happiness Enjoyment Blueprint workshop**.

Some of you who might relate to the skills and habits mentioned in this chapter/book with ideal qualities required for overall wellbeing.

So here we go for mastering the art and science of living a happy life.

1. The first step in living a happy life is learning the art of Mindful Meditation.

What is Mindful Meditation?
The words meditation and mindfulness are well known to most people. However, the term mindful meditation is not known to all, as it is a new concept of fusion of meditation and mindfulness.

T Harv Eker, a famous author, businessman, and motivational speaker from who I have taken lessons through an online training program on Mastering Happiness, states that Happiness is natural. You are already happy until you make yourself unhappy."

I perfectly agree with him and have also experienced the same. Hence, I have created Mindful Meditation as the first step of living a happy life.

Let us first understand meditation and mindfulness before we do its fusion to create our Happiness.

What is Meditation?

Meditation is a technique to observe your thoughts without passing any judgment on your thoughts. You become a silent observer of your thoughts. We cannot stop the thoughts from entering the mind, but we can certainly let the thoughts come and go.

Why should we meditate?

Since we cannot control the entry of thoughts, most of us get controlled by the thoughts, and the negative thoughts can cause agitations and disturbance in the mind.

These agitations in minds start after we entertain the negative thoughts. Hence, we do not react with negative thoughts. When our negative thoughts don't get attention, our mind remains calm and serene.

A calm and serene mind is the first stepping stone to creating happiness.

If you meditate on any symbol of your choice, all your thoughts get focused on it, and your mind gets engrossed in the symbol without entertaining any other thoughts.

One big advantage of meditation is it brings our mind to the present moment without worrying about the past or dreaming about the future.

Some of you may also feel the existence of yourself as a part of the entire universe. You will not identify your individual existence after experiencing this state of mind as you remain united with the Universe and the Creator of Universe, i.e., God.

This is the point where we realize our Higher Self which is powerful, full of bliss, and always succeeds. If you can learn to stay in this state of mind, you can also imbibe the super qualities of the Higher Self and distance yourself from one big enemy of happiness, i.e., the lower self.

The main reason for meditation is to prepare our mind for happiness by giving it freedom from stress and anxiety originating from the demanding life and busy schedules full of workloads.

How to Meditate?

Meditation is very simple and can be done with zero types of equipment. You neither have to go to the Himalayas nor to dense forests to meditate. You don't even have to buy costly equipment to meditate.

Let's learn to meditate as a skill as well as a habit.

From the skill point, one needs to sit in a quiet place of one's choice, close one's eyes, and focus on any symbol or object one likes the most. Once one fix one's eyes on the symbol/object, one starts observing one's breath which one inhales and exhales. So, one uses the symbol/object for focusing one's minds on it, and thereafter one stands observing one's breath. This helps one to stay focused on it for a longer duration.

If one does meditation by sitting in a Padmasana (Yoga posture), then one can fetch better results.

Where should we meditate?

We hardly find a quiet place in our busy life surrounded by a complex noise polluted world. Not finding a quiet place should not be an excuse for not doing meditation. One can do meditation at any place and even during one's waiting period also for e.g., when one is stuck in traffic or traveling on a train or a plane or even while during one's routine activities (with eyes wide open). What I am trying to say is meditation is a natural activity like breathing and eating. One needs to learn the art of focusing one's mind on stopping entertaining negative thoughts and preparing the mind for one's next step of happiness, i.e., Mindfulness.

When should you meditate?

From the habit point of view, one should learn to meditate after one wakes up in the morning and before one goes to bed at night.

In addition to these two important times during the day, one should also meditate as and when one gets an opportunity to meditate.

What are the benefits of meditation?

1. Meditation frees the mind from stress and anxiety.

2. Meditation makes one aware of one's real Higher Self.

3. One can experience the super qualities of the Higher Self with meditation.

4. Meditation prepares you for mindfulness and helps you to give directions for positive emotions.

5. Meditation develops a fire-wall (in terms of cyber security) or a strong chakra view that cannot be broken or penetrated by any of the enemies of happiness.

What is Mindfulness?

One can bring one's mind to its natural calm and serene state with meditation. One can slow down the thoughts and try to reach zero thought levels. But our purpose of meditation is not to sit like yogis on the mountains for years together. We need to play our role and perform our daily activities.

Mindfulness will help us to direct our thoughts to the activity on hand. Mindfulness helps us to fully engage our thoughts in the present moment and ensure that no entry is provided to negative thoughts.

In meditation, one focuses one's attention on a symbol or object for letting the thoughts come and go without entertaining the thoughts. However, in Mindfulness, we let the thoughts originate that are directed towards our goal and purpose of life.

In meditation, one concentrates on a symbol or object. In Mindfulness, we become aware of our goal and direct our thoughts towards it.

5 seconds habit of mindfulness

Once your mind is calm and peaceful with meditation, you need to prioritize your thoughts on the planned activity. This prioritization of thoughts can be instantly done in 5 seconds. Focus on your Higher Self and make the following affirmation.

"I want to be happy. Hey peaceful mind, please concentrate all my positive thoughts on the activity on hand."

I have successfully practiced it. You, too, can also do it.

Why Mindfulness?

The basic problem with one's mind is it has the freedom to travel from the past to the present and from the present to the future as a time machine. But we cannot do so as we have to be in the present for doing the activity on hand. Action originates from thoughts and feelings. Hence if we have to succeed in our action, we need to direct our thoughts and feelings towards the activity on hand to succeed and produce good results.

If we permit our mind to wander between past and future, it will surround us with stress and the anxiety about the future. Due to stress and anxiety, our minds will be filled with negative energy, which will not let us concentrate on the activity on hand. The negative energy will deplete and exhaust our positive energy, and we will either postpone the activity on hand or simply give away the activity on hand. This will result in inefficiency and failure in our day-to-day activities.

Hence mindfulness helps us to first become aware of the activity on hand based on the vision and goals of our life and direct 100% energy towards achieving our goals.

Many people spend their precious time in life in autopilot mode by surrendering themselves to the jumping mind and dancing to its tunes. They are neither aware of their potential nor their life goals.

Mindfulness can certainly help all people to become productive in their activities by directing 100% energy towards meeting their goals. Once one succeeds in one's activities, happiness will automatically flow from it, and one's hard work will be rewarded.

How to practice Mindfulness?

The first step in Mindfulness is to become aware of the situation and circumstances faced by you.

The second step in Mindfulness is to become aware of the purpose in doing anything in the present moment. One should then rewire one's brain by directing one's thoughts to do actions based on the current situation and circumstances. One's brain should be clear as to what steps need to be taken for completing the task on hand.

With the first two steps, one perceives things, directs one's thoughts to the activity on hand, and then manage the activity on hand till its completion.

One directs one's brain to remain committed till the activity on hand is completed. Similarly, one should also remain committed to the completion of the activity without falling prey to any distractions.

We can develop simple habits to do our daily activities mindfully as follows:

Mindful Eating

If one pays attention to the food, one eats and does not just swallow the food, one will create happiness for one's stomach. One's food will get digested properly, and all the vitamins and minerals would be easily absorbed by the body.

If one can breathe properly during eating and feel the food passing through one's nicely salivated mouth, one will savor the food one eats.

Mindful Exercise

One should be clear with what activities one is going to do at a fixed time. It can include a warm-up exercise; it can have weight lifting, stretching, sprinting, cycling, etc. Whatever one does, one should continue to breathe and note the changes that are happening in one's body. One needs to pick up the intensity and get into a rhythm. At the end of the exercise, one needs to cool down and relax. Every part of the exercise has a purpose and needs to be done mindfully for getting the results rather than doing the exercise haphazardly.

Mindful Driving

Driving has to be done with care and safety. A small mistake can cost very dearly. When one's vehicle is on the road, and one is stuck in traffic, the person is on their own to deal with the situation. So are other drivers. Some drivers prefer to horn and create noise pollution, while others prefer to sulk in the car and get frustrated because of traffic.

A mindful person will do deep breathing to pump in more oxygen in the body and rejuvenate himself rather than feeling stressed.

The next thing he/she will do is to import positive emotions to feel at ease and relax. If required, he/she may have a small sip of juice or water kept in the car for such an occasion and also feed himself/herself with some light snacks. Now he/she will look around and note that all other drivers are also facing the same traffic problem. However, their approach is different, and they are stressed. The calm and positive mind will convince you to use your time to browse some eBooks, watch the news, listen to favorite song albums so that you don't feel the wait but mindfully utilize your time doing useful activities rather than getting frustrated.

Having understood the meaning and application of Meditation and Mindfulness, now let us understand what exactly Mindful Meditation is.

Mindful Meditation will help you to calm down your mind and remain focused on the activity on hand, and do all the necessary things required for completion of the activity as per the goal or purpose.

One should learn to fully focus one's attention on the present moment without worrying about the past regrets or anxiety about the future.

Mindful Meditation can reduce your stress, improve your concentration, keep you fit and healthy to perform your task, and ensure completion with grit and resilience.

One can practice mindful Meditation in one's daily activities and make the best use of every moment to remain happy and productive.

2. Positive emotions

After understanding the power of mindful meditation, one is ready to take up any assignment and challenges with a calm and focused mind.

Just like a tree cannot survive without manure, water, fertilizers and insecticides, a human being also requires the help of positive emotions to inspire them to perform all the actions for completion of activities as per their goal and vision.

While doing one's activities, one will face various challenges under different situations and circumstances. However, positive emotions help us to look at the brighter side of life for getting better results.

One may not get ideal situations all the time. But positive emotions motivate us to make the most of difficult situations with a positive outlook.

Some of the popular positive emotions that are used by happy people are as follows:

Joy: Joy is experienced when one is elated due to success or good fortune. Some people believe that the emotion of joy is grander than pleasure.

Gratitude: One appreciates and thanks to someone for the good things done for them by someone.

Serenity: Meditation makes your mind calm and serene. Serenity manifests peace and tranquility. The serenity can be observed in water in a pond until ripples are created due to some disturbance created on the surface of the water.

Hope: A person with a positive mindset desires a good outcome from the activities in the present or in the future. Hope motivates the person to act rather than remain dejected and frustrated.

Amusement: Amusement can happen due to poking of fun or humor to provide a small pleasure. Amusement can lighten up a matter and flash a smile on the person to pull out of some stress.

Inspiration: Inspiration is a feeling which provides a stimulus to a person to get motivated to do or create something fabulous.

Awe: Awe expresses the surprise or wonder after experiencing a grand and spectacular outcome.

Altruism: Altruism is a feeling that creates a desire to do an act for others and become happy when they succeed. The best part of altruism is selflessness and unselfish concern for other people.

Satisfaction: Satisfaction is a feeling evoked after one's needs are fulfilled, or one's expectations are met. A satisfied person derives a small pleasure from the fulfillment of needs or meeting of expectations.

Relief: Relief is a relaxing feeling when one finds oneself saved or surviving an uncertain situation and avoiding a negative outcome.

Love and Affection: Love and Affection is a feeling of emotional attachment towards someone or something and going to any extent in providing all the good things in life to the person or thing one loves.

Cheerfulness: Cheerfulness brightens up one's face with optimism and upbeat due to something happening exactly the way one wants.

Confidence: Confidence evokes a strong belief in oneself and raises one's self-esteem so that one is prepared to do any task with ease and courage.

Enthusiasm: Enthusiasm displays a strong sense of interest and excitement to do a particular activity and remain engaged with it.

Euphoria: Euphoria is experienced when some surprising act or action beyond imagination has happened. It automatically makes the person happy due to the unraveling of something intense and exciting.

Contentment: Contentment is a feeling to be happy with what you have, who you are, and where you are.

Enjoyment: Enjoyment is a process of taking pleasure or benefit from activities, situations, or circumstances

Optimism: Optimism is a belief that something happening in the future will be good.

Why Positive emotions?

We are gifted with both positive and negative emotions to make the best use of them for creating and enjoying happiness.

Negative emotions like anger, fear, etc., help us to fight or protect ourselves from danger. They also help us to sharpen our focus on threats and vulnerabilities in our daily activities.

"A pessimist sees the difficulty in every opportunity; an optimist sees the opportunity in every difficulty."

-Winston Churchill

Positive emotions inspire us to seek hedonic pleasures and make life worth living. Positive emotions can help us to broaden our ideas, improve our performance and well-being with minimal or zero stress.

The moment you have a negative emotion entering into your mind without permission, visualize your Higher Self for the first three seconds. In the next two seconds, bring back the focus on your planned activity by saying the following affirmation in the mind.

"Hey obedient mind, please realize the qualities of the Higher Self and think with positive thoughts. I am a part of the Higher Self, and you should also think like the Higher Self."

Finally, in the remaining two seconds, bring in the desired positive emotion and put it into the planned activity. I have successfully practiced it. You, too, can do it.

One cannot ignore negative emotions or rely only on positive emotions. One needs to use a mix of positive and negative emotions to succeed in life and enjoy happiness.

Positive emotions can provide various benefits such as:

- ✓ Improve memory and concentration
- ✓ Increase our attention span and thinking abilities
- ✓ Enhance mental satisfaction
- ✓ Improve relationships
- ✓ Generate higher productivity
- ✓ Higher job satisfaction
- ✓ Foster Resilience
- ✓ Transform a person into a leader
- ✓ Build intellectual prowess and improve social skills
- ✓ Make the person a better team player

How to emote and elicit positive emotions in 10 seconds?

Positive emotions can be emoted instantly with some practice. If you want to succeed in instantly converting unhappy feelings into happy, positive emotions within 10 seconds follow my simple and easy technique.

Simple and easy technique to convert unhappy feelings into positive emotions within 10 seconds:

First 3 seconds: Experience the Higher Self with a 3-minute meditation.

Next 3 seconds: Make an affirmation 3 times: "My original nature is happiness."

Next 3 seconds: Feel a positive emotion that will help you to see good things even in an unhappy situation.

Final second: Immerse yourself in the positive feeling.

Once you succeed in creating positive emotions and start enjoying benefits from your action, you will be leveraging excellent advantages from it.

Positive affirmations: Start your day with positive affirmations wishing good things to happen rather than pouncing on the WhatsApp or newspapers.

List of positive affirmations:

"I can do any good thing and succeed in it."

"I am grateful for the opportunity I am getting and enjoy doing it."

"I will always complete my tasks and excel in it."

<u>Goal setting</u>: The first step to emote positive emotion is to be clear with one's goal

<u>Be optimistic</u>: Visualize yourself to succeed in your plans and pay attention to positive things rather than negative thoughts.

"Optimism is a strategy for making a better future. Because unless you believe that the future can be better, you are unlikely to step up and take responsibility for making it so."

-Noam Chomsky

<u>Generate enthusiasm</u>: Generate enthusiasm to strongly believe in one's success in every small activity one does.

<u>Practice mindful meditation</u>: Practice mindful meditation to focus one's thoughts on the activity on hand.

Don't let negative emotions disturb the flow, by reframing the negative thought with positive substitutes. Keep yourself relaxed by listening to some soothing music.

Challenge oneself: Challenge oneself to remain positive in all situations and circumstances. Eat healthily and have a good sleep.

Practice Gratitude: Practice Gratitude to tap the energies of the higher self and downplay the ego of the lower self.

There is a possibility that one may miss some steps initially—the best way to reinforce this technique is to write it down in the gratitude journal daily. Remember to include the Awe moments in your gratitude journal.

When to emote or elicit positive emotions?

Positive emotions are to be emoted for creating positive experiences. Since we want to be happy every moment, positive emotions should also be emoted every moment.

Positive emotions will enliven our skills and keep us prepared to face any situation and circumstance and eventually help us to succeed in every activity and become happy.

Positive emotion is a central concept for happiness. One can easily train their brains with simple habits to generate positive thoughts while they are engaged in positive activities.

3. Flow

The word Flow was coined and popularized by famous Positive Psychologist Mihaly Csikszentmihalyi.

Flow is a state of mind in which the person is fully engaged and immersed in his activity. In the state of Flow, the person thoroughly enjoys his activity and becomes more creative, productive, and happy in the present moment.

A person in a flow works with greater enthusiasm and makes the best use of his skills.

While doing the work in a flow, a person ensures that he contributes non-stop efforts without giving priority to hunger, time spent, or whether others are contributing their efforts to the work or not. Such a person puts in a single-minded effort and corrects himself with self-feedback to work persistently till the work is completed.

The concept of Flow is a perfect fit for the first two steps, i.e., mindful meditation and positive emotions for living a happy life.

Why Flow?

Mindful Meditation and Positive Emotions will prepare one's mind and engage one's mind to perform an activity as per one's goal. But there are higher chances of some breaks in their activities due to sudden distractions. However, if the persons learn to be in flow, then they won't be affected by any distractions and can remain fully engaged in their activities till completion.

The concept of flow can cause improved performance in various domains.

How to be in flow?

The first step to being in flow is to set clear goals on what one wants to achieve. Then one needs to choose an activity one loves the most. Sometimes you may have to do an activity for the welfare of the team. In such a case, substitute your negative emotions with positive emotions and remind your mind of your responsibility to perform your role.

Identify the trigger, which prepares you to enter into the state of flow. The trigger factor can be your expertise in skills, your passion for helping people, or a sense of excellent teamwork.

Once you enter into the state of flow, have intense focus and pay attention to any signals you get in the form of feedback to refine your approach and improve your efforts.

4.Responsible and Accountable (Responsibility Accounting)

"Your heart, your life, your happiness is your responsibility and your responsibility alone."

-Will Smith

With Mindful Meditation, Positive Emotions, and being in Flow, you can master the art of being productive and successful in your activities.

However, human beings are not perfect and consistent. Something may go wrong initially until you master this art.

Hence, you need to have a framework of responsibility and accountability for your failures. It simply means you should take personal responsibility for your mistakes and not blame others for your failures and unhappiness.

Many people think that happiness is enjoyed in the future and there is no deadline for it. Because of this casual attitude, people don't try to improve. Improvement can happen only with responsibility accounting. Only when one owns their mistake will they try to correct it and improve.

Responsibility Accounting is a very important aspect in creating happiness and enjoying it for a longer duration.

Be responsible for your actions, and learn to walk the happiness path and access happiness every moment.

5. Resilience

Well, now we have a complete framework of how to live a happy life. But what happens when you are stroked with a sudden disaster like the Covid pandemic or similar disasters.

Now, this is not your fault. You cannot blame for the slowdown or the lockdown. You have to learn to find your way in all situations and circumstances.

Our approach and mindset can decide the outcome of happiness.

So, here again, we have a solution. We can deal with small and big setbacks or disasters with the art of Resiliency.

What is Resilience?

Resilience helps an individual to quickly recover from difficult situations and bounce back to bring back life to normal levels after a struggle.

"Resilience is accepting your new reality, even if it's less good than the one you had before. You can fight it, you can do nothing but scream about what you've

lost, or you can accept that and try to put together something that's good."

-Elizabeth Edwards

The art of Resiliency helps the person to deal with adversity. Resilient people have mastered the skill to bounce back and rebuild their lives after the struggle.

Resilient people make the best use of their resources and strengths to cope with adversities, difficulties, and hardships to face the challenges and come out of setbacks in life.

Generally, we use the word Resilience for bouncing back to achieve short-term goals. But when it comes to achieving long-term goals in the midst of disaster and difficulty, we use the word grit.

Grit involves continuing your interest and efforts for achieving long-term goals. Grit requires more self-control, willpower, discipline, and perseverance for sustaining mental toughness for a longer duration.

Both Grit and Resilience are important concepts for us to achieve both short-term and long-term happiness.

- ✓ The secret formula to happiness is to learn to live a happy life without even chasing to acquire more material possessions.
- ✓ You can easily discover your Happiness after becoming aware of yourself and living your life with a proper vision and goal.
- ✓ If you want to become a Happiness Conqueror, you need to find the right address of Happiness.
- ✓ Your Happiness depends entirely on your choice to be happy and the priority you give to your goal to be happy.
- ✓ The first step in living a happy life is learning the art of Mindful Meditation.
- ✓ Positive emotions inspire us to seek hedonic pleasures and make life worth living.
- ✓ In the state of Flow, the person thoroughly enjoys his activity and

becomes more creative, productive, and happy in the present moment.

✓ Resilient people make the best use of their resources and strengths to cope with adversities, difficulties, and hardships to face the challenges and come out of setbacks in life.

Chapter 8: Happiness Gems of All Chapters

Happiness Gems of Chapter 1: Introduction

- ✓ Start your journey of happiness by reading this book and learn to be always happy.

Happiness Gems of Chapter 2: Why should we discover and conquer the enemies of Happiness?

- ✓ The enemies of happiness start attacking us, and we begin the most extensive search of our life: to identify the worst enemies of our happiness.

✓ Since we cannot get a clear answer from anyone, we have to find the answers to our happiness questions by ourselves.

✓ We do succeed in getting some good answers to this big question of our life.

✓ Our intense and hectic schedule forces us to get back to work until the same or new enemy of happiness once again strikes us and makes us unhappy.

✓ The pursuit of happiness becomes more complex with more achievement – be it wealth, status, promotion, success, comforts, luxuries etc

✓ With a focused approach and a mindful thinking, I have succeeded in conquering the enemies of happiness.

✓ You should have no worries now about the enemies of happiness, as I am going to share my secrets, techniques, tools, strategies and tactics to become happy every moment, irrespective of, in what situation, circumstances you are in and WITHOUT spending a bomb on costly consultations and programs.

- ✓ Your search for long lasting happiness is now over, as I am going to manifest a simple and easy step-by-step approach to become happy and stay happy for as long as you want.
- ✓ I will teach you everything about happiness, including the what, why, how, where, when, who and which of happiness essential for earning the precious designation of a happiness conqueror.

Happiness Gems of Chapter 3: What is Happiness?

- ✓ Happiness is a choice for every human being.
- ✓ Every human being can enjoy his natural state of happiness, until he does something silly that makes him unhappy.
- ✓ Happiness is a feeling which is experienced within, and determined by one's state of mind.

- ✓ Happiness has two extremes in ecstasy on one end and frustration on the other end.
- ✓ In the neutral state, we are neither pleased nor frustrated and still claim to be happy.
- ✓ A happier person knows the right way to dilute the impact of negative emotions and challenges and succeeds in every situation and circumstances to enjoy happiness every moment.
- ✓ Every entity has its own way to perceive happiness and enjoy happiness.
- ✓ We cannot be happy by living in comparisons, but by living in the present moment and enjoying the present moment.
- ✓ Happiness is our birth-right as we are all born happy.
- ✓ Happiness is expressed in different ways by different schools of thought.
- ✓ Even though the external factors can provide us pleasure and generate the happiness hormones within ourselves, we can generate the happiness

hormones without the external materials.

✓ Long lasting happiness can be experienced with the help of specific positive emotions such as satisfaction and contentment.

✓ Happiness is the ultimate goal of our life and hence we should learn to be happy every moment.

Happiness Gems of Chapter 4: Who are the Enemies of Happiness?

✓ We should prioritize listing all these causes of disturbance of peace and happiness and call them enemies of joy. Once we make a list of happiness enemies, we should attack them one at a time so that our focus becomes very strong against these enemies. Since we attack them one at a time, each enemy becomes the No. 1 enemy for that moment of attack.

✓ Five worst enemies of happiness: 1. Jumping Mind 2. Ego 3. Fear 4. Anger 5. Greed.

- ✓ Weapon to destroy the Jumping Mind: Transform your Jumping Mind to Mindful Mind.
- ✓ Weapon to destroy the Self-centred Ego: Transform the Self-centred Ego to Self-less Ego.
- ✓ Weapon to destroy the Fear: Reframe the fearful thoughts and focus on your activity which you can perform with your knowledge, skills and abilities.
- ✓ Weapon to destroy Anger: Forgive others for their misdeeds and let go of the negative emotions. Practice gratitude and thank God for what he has given and get going with the situation.
- ✓ Weapon to destroy Greed: Live a minimalist life full of contentment, satisfaction, gratitude, generosity and acquire your essentials rather than running after non-essential things.

Happiness Gems of Chapter 5: Simple lies about Happiness

- ✓ Simple lies about happiness can also be called Myths about Happiness.

Myths are beliefs made by people and established over a while.

- ✓ Happiness depends upon people's perception, someday, someone may find a deeper meaning and discover the falsity of the myth.
- ✓ Some myths about happiness may give us a wrong notion of becoming happy, while other tales may make us feel miserable.
- ✓ It is essential to understand the meaning behind the myths and blend their usefulness with our journey of true happiness.
- ✓ Myth number 1: Happiness is naturally available for human beings.
- ✓ Myth number 2: Happiness depends upon success in achieving material gains.
- ✓ Myth number 3: Happiness is a destination and not a journey.
- ✓ Myth number 4: Children are happier than grown-ups and elders.
- ✓ Myth number 5: Happiness comes by luck and chance.
- ✓ Myth number 6: Happiness comes from external material pleasures.

- ✓ Myth number 7: Happiness is outside in rather than inside out.
- ✓ Myth number 8: A simple and minimalist life won't create happiness in life.
- ✓ Myth number 9: Your job or business will make you happy.
- ✓ Myth number 10: Happiness can be obtained with loneliness.
- ✓ Myth number 11: Surrender to nature and accept everything to become happy.
- ✓ Myth number 12: We are not happy because of someone else's fault.

Happiness Gems of Chapter 6: Simple truths about Happiness

- ✓ True Happiness can be experienced in both pleasure and pain.
- ✓ Happiness is a choice based on our perspective.
- ✓ Self-Awareness can lead to Happiness
- ✓ Happiness increases by giving happiness to others.
- ✓ Everyone can be happy at all times.

✓ Happier people succeed in life but successful people may not be happy.
✓ Happiness can be found by connecting with nature.
✓ Good relationships can make you happy.
✓ Happy people consciously use positive thoughts by identifying with the Higher Self.
✓ Happiness is experienced while working towards the goal.
✓ A wise man is spontaneously happy.
✓ A strong determination to be happy will always make you happy.

Happiness Gems of Chapter 7: How to live a Happy life?

✓ The secret formula to happiness is to learn to live a happy life without even chasing to acquire more material possessions.
✓ You can easily discover your Happiness after becoming aware of yourself and living your life with a proper vision and goal.

- ✓ If you want to become a Happiness Conqueror, you need to find the right address of Happiness.
- ✓ Your Happiness depends entirely on your choice to be happy and the priority you give to your goal to be happy.
- ✓ The first step in living a happy life is learning the art of Mindful Meditation.
- ✓ Positive emotions inspire us to seek hedonic pleasures and make life worth living.
- ✓ In the state of Flow, the person thoroughly enjoys his activity and becomes more creative, productive, and happy in the present moment.
- ✓ Resilient people make the best use of their resources and strengths to cope with adversity, difficulties, and hardships to face the challenges and come out of setbacks in life.

Do you want to share your story/conduct workshops at your workplaces or even schools, colleges, and educational institutions / get further guidance from me?

<u>Happiness Updates</u>

I have tried to unravel all the secrets of happiness available to me. However, life keeps on changing for both you and me. We gather more experience in our journey of happiness.

Sharing the updated knowledge & wisdom that I gain as I progress in life is my passion. I am sure you will love to know more about the updated secrets from me from my website, https://www.ebookswritingtoearnmoney.com

Happiness success Stories

Similarly, I will love to hear happiness success stories from you by reading my book. Remember your experience can become a great inspiration for others. We have already learned that happiness increases by sharing. Your happiness success story will also help me learn from your experience and invent new techniques to enrich this book further. I will be glad to include your stories in the next edition of my book by giving your name credits.

You can also suggest a specific aspect of happiness you want me to write my next book. You can send a personal email to me at **happinessmastery@gmail.com**

If you want to invite me to conduct in-house workshops/seminars/webinars at/for your workplaces or even schools, colleges, and educational institutions, you can send me your inquiry/requirement at **happinessmastery@gmail.com**. I can also design a customized happiness program, suiting the needs of a specific kind of audience.

Readers can achieve success in sustaining long-lasting happiness by staying connected. I invite you to stay connected with me to share your happiness success stories, suggest specific aspects of happiness you want me to write my next book, and also get future updates about my projects.

Join my 3 Days Happiness Enjoyment Program

Connect on **happinessmastery@gmail.com** to get more details about the 3 Days Happiness Enjoyment Program

My second must read book on Happiness

https://www.ebookswritingtoearnmoney.com/post/happiness-for-all-age-groups-in-short-and-crisp-prescriptions

References Books

1. The Art of Happiness by Dalai Lama

2. Authentic Happiness by Martin Seligman

3. The Happiness Advantage by Shawn Achor

4. The How of Happiness by Sonja Lyubomirsky

5. The Happiness Trap by Dr. Russ Harris

6. Happiness in Hard Times by Andrew Matthews

7. How to be Happy all the time by Paramania Yoga Nanda

8. Pursuit of Happiness by Swami Chinmayananda

9. Being Happy by Swami Tejomayananda

10. Storm to Perform by Swami Swaroopananda

11. Governing Business and Relationship by A. Parthasarathy

12. Good Karma by Jaya Row

13. Happiness Unlimited by Sister B K Shivani

14. 7 mindsets of success, happiness and fulfilment by Swami Mukundananda

15. Happiness Unlimited by Swami Bodhananda

16. The Happiness Project by Gretchen Rubin

17. A guide to Total Happiness by Rima Rudner

18. Build Happier Brain by Som Bathla

19. The Happiness Equation by Neil Pasricha

20. Happiness Express by Khurshed Batliwala and Dinesh Ghodke

21. Happiness Hacks by Alex Palmer

22. Stumbling on Happiness by Daniel Gilbert

23.A little book on Happiness by Ruskin Bond

24.Delivering Happiness by Tony Hsieh

25.Mastering Happiness by Joel F Wade

26.Practising Happiness by Ruth A. Baer

27. Steps to find inner peace and happiness by Mike McCallister

28. How to be happy every single day by Nate Nicholson

29.Introducing Happiness A practical guide by Will Bukingham

30.The truth about happiness by Pran Saikia

Reference Websites

1.https://en.wikipedia.org/wiki/Happiness#Definitio
ns

2.https://en.wikipedia.org/wiki/Philosophy_of_happ
iness

3.https://en.wikipedia.org/wiki/%C4%80nanda_(Hin
du_philosophy)

4. https://www.vridhamma.org/discourses/The-
Meaning-of-Happiness

5. http://www.forastateofhappiness.com/tag/50-10-
40-formula

6. https://www.simplypsychology.org/maslow.html

7. https://www.pursuit-of-happiness.org/history-of-
happiness/martin-seligman-psychology

8. https://ppc.sas.upenn.edu/learn-more/perma-
theory-well-being-and-perma-workshops

9. https://www.authentichappiness.sas.upenn.edu

10. https://www.pursuit-of-happiness.org/history-
of-happiness/barb-fredrickson

11 https://thestorytellers.com/the-businessman-
and-the-fisherman

12. https://www.psychologytoday.com

13. https://www.psychologytoday.com

14. https://www.verywellmind.com

15. https://www.healthline.com

16. https://www.mayoclinic.org

17. https://www.crosswalk.com

18. https://www.goodreads.com

19. https://www.brainyquote.com

20. https://bestlifeonline.com

21. https://thehappinesstrap.com

22. https://www.happify.com

23. https://pursuit.unimelb.edu.au/podcasts

24. https://www.huffpost.com

25. https://www.betterup.com

26. https://happinesson.com

27. https://www.livehappy.com

28. https://www.livehappy.com

29. https://www.lifehack.org

30. https://www.prevention.com